The Master Cheesemakers

OF WISCONSIN

merry christmas
buddy.
love, chloe.
2009.

PUBLICATION OF THIS VOLUME
HAS BEEN MADE POSSIBLE, IN PART, THROUGH SUPPORT FROM THE

Wisconsin Milk Marketing Board, Inc.

and the

dairy farm families of Wisconsin.

The Master Cheesemakers

OF WISCONSIN

JAMES NORTON and BECCA DILLEY

THE UNIVERSITY OF WISCONSIN PRESS

The University of Wisconsin Press
1930 Monroe Street, 3rd Floor
Madison, Wisconsin 53711-2059

uwpress.wisc.edu

3 Henrietta Street
London WCE 8LU, England

5   4   3   2   1

Printed in Canada

Library of Congress Cataloging-in-Publication Data
Norton, James R.
The master cheesemakers of Wisconsin / James Norton and Becca Dilley.
p.   cm.
Includes bibliographical references and index.
ISBN 978-0-299-23434-8 (pbk. : alk. paper)
1. Cheesemakers—Wisconsin. 2. Cheese—Varieties—Wisconsin.
3. Cheesemaking—Wisconsin. I. Dilley, Becca. II. Title.
SF274.U6.N67   2009
637′.309775—dc22
2009009422

To all of

WISCONSIN'S MASTER CHEESEMAKERS

whatever their century or decade

CONTENTS

PREFACE

This book was born from more than a mere love of Wisconsin cheese. It also sprang from a deep-seated conviction that Wisconsin's master cheesemakers would be incredibly fun guys to get to know. The very phrase "Wisconsin cheesemaker" is one of those rare, perfect, euphonious expressions that leave you feeling inexplicably pleased after you hear them.

What's a Wisconsin cheesemaker like? Without having met any, you might say "jolly," or "hard-working," or "smelling somewhat of cooked milk." And all of these were true, more or less, of the various folks we met. But it was a search for other attributes—the subtle, intuitive grasp of math and biology, the fierce dedication to consistent quality in a profession dominated by fickle and living ingredients, and a simultaneous dedication to tradition and progress. It was that search that drove this book.

That search, in turn, led us to spend four months crisscrossing Wisconsin in our Honda Civic to meet—on his or her home turf—every active master cheesemaker who would meet with us. The fruits of those dozens of interviews, photo sessions, and cheese tastings are presented to you here, in these pages.

Güten Appetit!

ACKNOWLEDGMENTS

The authors would like to thank—first and foremost—the master cheesemakers of Wisconsin. Across the board, they were happy to meet with us, generous with their time, and gracious to a fault. Getting to meet them was a reward unto itself. Heather Porter Engwall and Patrick Geoghegan of the Wisconsin Milk Marketing Board were absolutely instrumental in making this book happen. Cathy Hart of the WMMB was fantastically patient and helpful under the onslaught of our cheesemaker-related inquiries. We can't thank WMMB enough for its financial, moral, logistical, and informational support. Jeanne Carpenter and her blog (www.cheeseunderground.com) were terrific resources for us. Thanks, Jeanne—keep blogging! Marianne Smukowski lined up a four-hour block of interviews with her colleagues at the Center for Dairy Research of the University of Wisconsin–Madison that was extremely instructive, if exhausting. We're grateful to her and all those who took the time to talk with us: Bill Wendorff, Mark Johnson, John Jaeggi, Dean Sommer, Joanne Gauthier, and Rusty Bishop. Jim Path gave us an hour-plus interview that put us on the right path in terms of the master cheesemaker program, and we're very grateful. John Fox gave us a place to stay in Cedarburg, Wisconsin, twice, and taught us about string cheese sauce. Josiah and Ingrid Dilley gave us a home-away-from-home for the seemingly dozens of visits we made to the Madison and Green County area. Cheesemonger/journalist Stephanie Lucianovic gave us an initial dose of encouragement that put us over the top, and we're grateful to her, and to Cowgirl Creamery, the San Francisco cheese shop that planted the initial seed from which this book sprouted. And we appreciate all that Raphael Kadushin, Sheila Moermond, and Terry Emmrich did to transform this book from a pile of raw text into the bound volume that you now hold in your hands.

The Master Cheesemakers

OF WISCONSIN

Introduction

WE DO NOT INTEND FOR THIS BOOK to be any sort of definitive work on the art and craft of cheesemaking. The authors were humbled by the knowledge of the cheesemakers, who were humbled by the knowledge of the staff at the Center for Dairy Research, who were humbled by the complicated and cantankerous living organisms that are known as "milk" and "cheese."

Up to a certain point, gaining knowledge about cheese only exposes how little you actually know about it. Later, that presumably becomes less true, but if any cheesemakers or scientists we spoke to had reached it, they were too modest or sly to say so.

It is obvious beyond stating that cheese is part of the soul of Wisconsin. It's easy enough to rattle off economic statistics that illustrate the significance of the dairy industry, but that misses the essential way that cheese shaped and defined the state over the years. Once upon a time, cheese was part of the frontier farmstead life; European immigrants, looking for a way to make milk last longer and create a tradable commodity, would turn out small batches. Usually, it was the wife who made the cheese, as the husband worked the fields. But a steep decline in wheat production in the 1870s made cheese an attractive economic alternative to grain and shifted the dairy industry to the forefront. As Jerry Apps notes in *Cheese: The Making of a Wisconsin Tradition*, the departure of cheese from the woman's domain was a welcome shift. Mrs. E. P. Allerton, speaking at the third annual meeting of the Wisconsin Dairymen's Association, said, "In many farmhouses, the dairy work loomed up every year, a mountain that it took all summer to scale. But the mountain is removed; it has been hauled over to the cheese factory."

Wisconsin dairy increasingly became a way to prosper, and cheese plants sprang up at almost every rural crossroads, pooling the milk and other resources of five or ten farmers. Milk couldn't travel far by wagon-hauled bottle, so plants were everywhere you looked; by 1922, nearly three thousand dotted the state's countryside. In the

3

first half of the twentieth century, better roads and the advent of the modern refrigerated bulk milk truck brought about bigger plants. Little crossroads plants shut down or consolidated, and plants with dozens of workers became increasingly common.

"There was a plant just about a mile down the road from my mom and dad's house, which they still live in," recalls Lynn Dairy's David Lindgren. "The plant is gone now—all the little plants have gone by the wayside as things have grown."

Time passed, and the national cheese exchange moved from Plymouth, Wisconsin, to Green Bay to the Chicago Mercantile Exchange. Family farms began to fold, and, with them, small cheese plants began to die or be consolidated into larger plants by the dozen. Commodity cheese on the large scale became the rule of the day, but before long states such as California began threatening to outproduce the Wisconsin dairy industry in terms of sheer volume. A crisis was at hand—the 1980s and early '90s were hard times, and many in the dairy industry got out.

The cheesemakers who remained were mostly working at large commodity plants (constantly in danger of buyout or closure) or small, often struggling old-fashioned plants making traditional Wisconsin cheese. Those who remained in the business were the tough, the hardy, the resourceful, and, increasingly, the insecure. "Sometimes you feel like you are one of the last people left," says David Metzig of the family-owned Union Star Cheese Factory. "You are the toughest, you survived—but maybe everyone else was smarter and you are the slowest one. It is a little of both," he adds with a laugh.

Stabilization came in the late '90s, as plant closures slowed down, and an increasing recognition of the unique artisan qualities of Wisconsin cheese began to be seen as a route to salvation for the industry. Wisconsin cheese, it was realized, was different. Wisconsin cheesemakers had been around for two, three, even four generations, making their product in a way that could be traced directly back to European traditions but was uniquely their own. Many Wisconsin cheesemakers were (and still are) living storehouses of decades of industry and artisan knowledge, something few other states could boast.

Specialty cheeses have grown from 4 percent of the cheese produced in the state to more than 16 percent in just a decade, according to a 2008 bulletin from the National Agricultural Statistics Service. Wisconsin now makes more than 35 percent of all specialty cheese sold in the United States. It also produces more than 600 varieties of cheese to California's 250, according to a 2007 story in the *Fresno Bee*.

"I gave a presentation on cheese, and people asked where the cheese came from," recalls Center for Dairy Research senior scientist Mark Johnson. "I said, 'These are all from Wisconsin,' and people thought I was joking. They thought they were imported. Every cheese you see imported we can make in Wisconsin. And make just as good, if not better because we have control over everything. The cheeses you get in Europe are great when they are made, but then you have to transport them."

The Center for Dairy Research

When the Center for Dairy Research was founded at the University of Wisconsin–Madison in 1986, it employed three people and was a glimmer of its future self. In 2008 the center employed more than thirty people, and now it exists as a unique crossroads between industry and academia, and theory and practical application.

In its current incarnation, the CDR is like a Jedi High Council of dairy knowledge. When a cheesemaker takes a problem to the CDR, it's very likely that one of its people will know the answer. If the CDR can't answer a question, it knows scientists who can research it, and—in the process—expand the frontiers of human knowledge.

The CDR, funded largely by the Wisconsin Milk Marketing Board and private industry, represents a place where industry can ask questions and find answers. It's a place where academics can find inspiration for research, and where research can give back to the state's economy. It's a storehouse of knowledge, constantly refreshed by constant contact with the real world.

Mention the CDR to a cheesemaker, and more often than not, his eyes will light up with respect. "Then we worked with the CDR" is what you tend to hear when you ask how a new cheese variety was developed, or how a particularly challenging problem was solved.

"I enjoy working with the people at CDR, and any opportunity I get to work with Mark Johnson or John Jaeggi or Marianne Smukowski," says master cheesemaker Roger Krohn. "You just learn so much from those people."

Despite its high standing in the dairy industry, the CDR maintains a low public profile.

"The CDR is probably the greatest unknown in the cheese industry today," says CDR researcher John Jaeggi. "We like to stay in the background because we strongly believe that the focus should be on those guys—the cheesemakers, the cheese companies, the ones in the trenches. So most people won't hear of us, but a lot of the award winners in cheese contests are a result of work done here."

The Wisconsin Master Cheesemaker Program

A joint effort sponsored by the Center for Dairy Research and the Wisconsin Milk Marketing Board, the Wisconsin Master Cheesemaker Program was envisioned as a way to acknowledge the immense depth of experience and talent that exists within the state's dairy industry. The CDR would put together courses to top off the specialized knowledge of the state's best cheesemakers, and the WMMB would use the Master's Mark (a trademark) as a way to market Wisconsin cheese and cheesemakers.

Before even applying to the program, applicants must have held their Wisconsin cheesemaking licenses for at least ten years. They must pass a strict oral exam from program board members, who are not easily fooled and fire questions at a fearsome rate.

Moreover, they must have been making the cheese variety for which they seek certification for five years. A cheesemaker picks one or two varieties of cheese to master in when entering the program; assuming a successful completion, he or she might emerge, for example, as a master of cheddar and asiago.

But to pass through and obtain the certificate and medal, a would-be master must take more than two years of courses, consent to constant testing of his cheese and evaluation of his plant, and—after all that—write an open-book final exam that can run to dozens of handwritten pages of answers.

The whole process runs somewhere between thirteen and fifteen years, including the initial runup to obtain a Wisconsin cheesemaker's license, no small feat unto itself.

Jim Path and the Masters

Originally conceived in the early '90s, the program was initially propelled and largely shaped by CDR specialty cheese expert Jim Path, who found inspiration across the Atlantic.

"I started making inquiries about master cheesemaker programs in Europe," he says. "We identified some programs in Europe—primarily the Swiss program. The Swiss had a good program, the Dutch had a program. . . . The Swiss definitely called theirs master cheesemaker, the Germans had a master cheesemaker . . . the Italians had a program. So in conjunction with the specialty program I traveled across Europe, and I visited schools. . . . It was fantastic. It was a dream come true. So we looked at the curriculums, and what became obvious was that some things fit and other things didn't."

The German program, for example, put students through intensive classroom and in-plant education before graduating them as master cheesemakers, at the age of twenty-one. Path, who came from a cheesemaking family, was interested in a program that celebrated and certified the time-tested cream of the crop—the veterans.

"We took that program and we looked at experienced cheesemakers; we said, 'OK, what are the criteria to be a master cheesemaker?'" he says. "You need a Wisconsin license. You need x number of years as an experienced, licensed cheesemaker. Then you need to go through some type of vocational courses and complete those courses and have some testing along the way."

In addition, the program's board evaluates the health and sanitation aspects of would-be masters' plants, and tests their cheese. Just constituting the board was a challenge—Path said there was a struggle to make it balanced.

"We tried to get a balance of big factories and small factories," he says.

The program was designed to further two goals.

"One was education, and that was our bailiwick at the Center for Dairy Research," Path says. "And the other was promotion, and that was WMMB. So basically, they took care of the promotion of the Wisconsin Master

Cheesemaker Program to promote Wisconsin cheeses, and we were involved in the educational aspect . . . and that was dear to my heart, and dear to the hearts of the cheesemakers who were involved."

Emeritus professor Bill Wendorff and senior scientist Mark Johnson of the CDR were also instrumental in making the program challenging for even the most experienced of cheesemakers, Path says. Path, for his part, put an emphasis on bringing European instructors to Wisconsin to teach old cheesemakers new tricks.

"We had just outstanding instructors come over," he says. "We'd spotlight cheeses from this or that particular country, and they'd do three or four cheeses. We'd have other microbiological seminars, process cheese seminars, so we built up a curriculum from nothing.

"In our first graduating classes we had large and we had small cheesemakers, and it had a lot of credibility," Path says. "I think the thing that really touched my heart a lot was they were on the young side. Now we see generational, where's there's been a master whose son is coming into the program. When you see generational, you say, 'Wow, that's really something.'"

Wendorff adds, "It's kind of like being a country doctor who delivers babies and watches them grow up and go through high school. You take a look at some of these guys and you see what they've done and you just feel good about how what you're doing in the program is really contributing toward that."

Walking through a Cheese Plant

Visitors and workers must suit up before walking the floor of a cheese plant. Hair nets and white coats (cloth or disposable) are required. In big plants, disposable earplugs are a must, often in tandem with safety glasses and slip-on paper booties for the feet.

Wherever you look there is a hose, sometimes underfoot, sometimes gushing into a vat or bucket or drain, sometimes coiled up, out of use, resting like a dormant snake. Cheese plants are places of humidity; it drips down glass, oozes across the floor, drains from vats, escapes from blocks of cheese placed in vacuum chambers; it is the key to certain aspects of cheesemaking, the bane of others. Antiseptic foam hisses quietly from nozzles near doorways, and the squishy tramp of shoes marching through a half-inch of surging white foam becomes one of the sounds a frequent cheese plant visitor learns to recognize.

At big plants, visitors are dwarfed by the scale. Holding or maturation tanks that hold tens of thousands of pounds of milk are not unusual. Closed vats can easily contain an automobile and, in some cases, a driveway to park it in. At small plants, visitors are impressed by the accessibility of the cheese; in embryonic form, it's close at hand, touchably close, curds and whey filling open vats. It sits in forms; it fills small cooling and aging and storage rooms, tantalizingly colorful and portable.

Stainless steel and white plastic predominate. If you go to a small artisan plant, there are curd knives and screens for cutting the curd to release additional whey, and forms that are filled by hand. Bigger plants have computer screens and, occasionally, robot arms that could easily crush a toolshed, but are employed, instead, to cut curd or move 640-pound blocks of cheese to where its masters would like it to be.

What Cheesemakers Are Like

Some cheesemakers are lean and wiry, most have big hands and broad shoulders, and some have a gut but are powerfully built nonetheless. In big factories, they are responsible for complicated "make" schedules,

TOURING WISCONSIN CHEESE PLANTS

Many of Wisconsin's master cheesemakers preside over large factory operations where tours aren't particularly practical. Fortunately, quite a few of the smaller and midsized operations allow and welcome visitors who might be curious about the state's dairy heritage.

If you're determined to see cheese being made, it's always best to call ahead. Some plants take a day or two off each week for maintenance, and cheese is often made only during specific hours of the day—typically before eleven in the morning.

Near Milwaukee / Fox Valley

Watching the team at Widmer's Cheese Cellars (Theresa) mat and mill their cheddar curd—or crank out old-fashioned brick—is a real Wisconsin treat. Joe Widmer is a consummate cheese showman, and his tiny shop doesn't overlook the action so much as it is surrounded by it. www.widmerscheese.com/ ph. (888) 878-1107

At Henning's Wisconsin Cheese (Kiel) visitors can view the plant through a picture window and tour a charming little cheese antiques museum. There's also a bustling retail operation that boasts some unique opportunities to sample master cheesemaker Kerry Henning's latest experiments. www.henningscheese.com/ ph. (920) 894-3032

In or Near Madison

Although the cheesemaking process isn't immediately on display at Cedar Grove Cheese (Plain), Robert Wills offers frequent tours and is happy to show off the plant's Living Machine. www.cedargrovecheese.com/ ph. (800) 200-6020

The Babcock Hall Dairy Plant is made for teaching, so it's quite accessible to the public. Self-guided tours can be arranged, and the Babcock Hall Dairy Store sells the plant's legendary ice cream and a variety of cheeses. www.foodsci.wisc.edu/services/dairy/ ph. (608) 263-2008

human resource decisions, the cost of milk and other ingredients, and the constant requests and complaints of customers. In small plants, they do all this plus electrical work, plumbing, carpentry, marketing, and more.

If you are looking for the antithesis of the modern, depressed, American office cubicle dweller, slumped over a PC loaded with a set of spreadsheets and Minesweeper, look no further than the master cheesemaker. Before eight in the morning, most have done more than an office worker does in a week.

Cheesemakers appear eerily young. A polite rule of thumb says that when you're guessing the age of a lady, deduct seven from your actual estimate; with cheesemakers, if you hope to actually guess the right age, you should probably add ten or fifteen years. I have met sixty-year-old cheesemakers who could twist me up into a pretzel and throw me into a well if it became absolutely necessary. And a lifetime of juggling variables and

Near Wisconsin Dells

Carr Valley Cheese Company has become rightfully famous for its selection of American Original cheeses that are unique to its plant. A small window offers a view of the plant. www.carrvalleycheese.com/ ph. (800) 462-7258

Near Wausau

The sprawling retail operation of Wisconsin Dairy State Cheese Company (Rudolph) boasts a big viewing window, tables and chairs, and an ice-cream shop. ph. (715) 435-3144

Near Minneapolis–St. Paul

Bass Lake Cheese Factory (Somerset) offers periodic wine and cheese tastings, an observation window, and an engaging, informal cheese heritage museum. Its store also boasts a selection of unique sheep and goat milk cheeses. www.blcheese.com/ ph. (715) 247-5586

Near Green Bay

At Union Star Cheese Factory (Zittau), David Metzig makes cheese the old-fashioned way, and sells some of the tastiest cheddar and string cheese in the state. www.unionstarcheese.com/ ph. (800) 354-3373

multitasking keeps the minds of cheesemakers sharp. Try spending a day worrying about acid levels, developing a new kind of aged cheddar laced with fruit, the amount of cheese in the warehouse, that recurring temperature problem with the pasteurizer (and the new guy who seems to be slacking off instead of working, of course), and see if you don't feel a little more mentally agile when you're through.

"They're all over the board, personally," says Jim Path. "One thing that they probably have in common is that they're extremely independent. Their personalities are all over the board, they vary from colorful"—here he chuckles—"to pretty methodical. They share a love of cheesemaking."

It seems sappy to observe that cheesemakers are good people, but it's impossible to avoid that conclusion.

"They're the kind of guys who, if you were on a sinking ship, would start tearing off doors and putting people on them," says Carie Wagner of Foremost Farms USA. "And then handing you a beer as you float off. 'You need a beverage!'"

They are accustomed to hard work, bred to share credit and shy away from the limelight, prone to handling problems by grabbing them head-on and wrestling them to the ground. There is very little glamour and only modest riches to be gained from making cheese twelve hours a day, five, six, or even seven days a week. Those who put up with the absurd hours, the heavy lifting, the economic pressure, and the smell of milk on their clothes and hair are the kind of people who think nothing of going a little bit out of their way to help another person deal with a problem.

The Cheesemaker's Life

The day-to-day life for a cheesemaker varies wildly. Some are preoccupied with smearing bacteria wash on aging wheels, and matting out cheddar curds. Others are using world-class science to troubleshoot minute aspects of a given cheese's performance in order to satisfy the demands of a customer who places orders by the millions of pounds. Most think about sales, marketing, human resources, sanitation, product development, labels, and equipment.

What master cheesemakers have in common, regardless of the size of their plants, is a soup-to-nuts understanding of their product, from the silage or grass eaten by the cows to the finished, often aged cheese eaten by consumers. The art of cheesemaking is less obvious when it's concealed by enormous closed vats and 640-pound-capacity wooden crates, but it's there. The challenge of making a consistent, delicious end product is a constant struggle regardless of the size of the operation in question.

Some masters are tinkerers, constantly changing recipes and playing with the milk, culture, and rennet in search of some wonderful undiscovered or long-forgotten cheese. Some are overseers of vast quantity, judging success on the movement of tractor-trailers of perfectly consistent cheese. But all of them are workhorses.

Making cheese is not for the lazy, or even the conventionally hard working. Twenty-four-hour plant cycles, off-peak electricity, milk delivery schedules, and a whole host of other reasons mean that many masters start their days at four in the morning, or three, or even two.

And if you're not juggling one of the dozens of fussy variables that go into making good cheese, you're probably working at one of the other jobs that are part of your "cheesemaker" title—engineer, CEO, foreman, janitor, cheerleader, accountant, or tour guide.

Only experience in multitasking, gained over time, can make a true master.

"Cheesemaking is like driving a car. When you first start, there is so much to watch—all the gauges, the temperature, what is this," says Dean Sommer, a CDR technologist. "You know the rules, and you can get down

How to Make Cheese, Briefly

Trying to describe how cheese is made is like trying to describe how a bakery makes everything that it sells. A cupcake, a croissant, a loaf of bread, and a chocolate chip cookie are all similar in many ways, but the make procedure varies considerably from one item to the next. If anything, cheese is even more variable—it's difficult to generalize beyond a few commonly practiced steps.

Cheese begins with milk. After that, things get complicated. In general, the milk is pasteurized and cooled—although there are raw milk cheeses, which are illegal for sale in the United States unless they've been aged for sixty days. Starter bacteria and rennet enzymes are then—generally—added to the pasteurized milk. The rennet separates the curd (which will become cheese) from the whey, which is siphoned off and either discarded or processed into a variety of dairy protein–related products. Whey can also be made into specialized cheeses, such as ricotta or gjetost.

The starter bacteria are allowed to work on the cheese-in-progress, changing its acidity and flavor profile. The bacteria's progress is carefully regulated by the cheesemaker, who uses a combination of salt, temperature, and curd cutting to control how rapidly the cheese evolves.

The curd can now be stacked and milled (cheddar), heated and pressed firmly (parmesan, asiago, emmental), injected and/or washed with ripening microbes over a course of hours or days (limburger, camembert, blue), pickled in brine (feta), heated and stretched (mozzarella, provolone), or washed in warm water and pressed (edam, gouda).

A variety of aging (affinage) techniques that can be applied to cheese include washing the cheese with beer or wine, rotating and/or flipping the cheese, or adjusting temperature and humidity levels in the aging room. The degree to which a cheese ages varies radically by variety. Some cheeses are best consumed almost immediately, or in the first few weeks of life, such as fresh mozzarella or mascarpone. Others, such as parmesan, provolone, or cheddar, are made to be aged and often reach a peak two, three, five, or even ten years after they're made. Cheesemakers tell tales of twenty- or even twenty-eight-year-old cheddars that are still edible, if not actually delicious.

the road, but you don't have the feel and the comfort level. That is the artistry, the comfort level. With cheesemaking, you don't have to watch the pH meter constantly; you can look and see and feel and know how it is going."

Mass-Produced versus Artisanal Cheese

While many master cheesemakers are full-fledged artisanal makers or utilize some artisanal methods of production, the line that separates large-scale commercial operations from small artisanal shops is far blurrier than it may initially look. It's impossible to say what precisely indicates an artisanal maker, but here are a few likely possibilities:

> An emphasis on quality over consistency
> Personal handling of the cheese (cutting the curd by hand, turning aging cheese by hand, filling forms
>   by hand)
> Small volume production (a few thousand pounds a day)
> Experimentation and the production of many different sorts of cheese, some seasonal, some one-offs
> The use of specialty milks (goat, sheep, pasture-grazed cow, certified organic)
> Sale to gourmet cheese shops, direct to public, high-end restaurants
> Using more (usually more specially trained) employees per pound of cheese produced.

By contrast, you could expect a plant emphasizing mass production to:

> Use only standard cow milk
> Produce only a few kinds of cheese
> Produce many thousands of pounds of cheese daily
> Rely on machines to stir curd and move cheese throughout the production cycle
> Sell large volumes of cheese for industrial food service or large grocery chain needs
> Emphasize a consistent product produced on an unvarying schedule
> Use fewer (usually more generally trained) employees per pound of cheese produced.

Few master cheesemakers fall squarely into either category, however. There are plants making small amounts of specialty cheese that use some automated equipment and no particularly special kinds of milk; there are huge plants concerned with making high-priced gourmet cheese or constantly experimenting with many new products. Most master cheesemakers have operations that fall somewhere along the spectrum between classic artisanal maker and full-fledged mass producer, without being completely on either end.

Regardless, every master cheesemaker knows the craft inside and out. No matter the size of the operation, the cheesemaker in charge needs to know every aspect of the process. At all levels of the game, things (often) go wrong in cheesemaking. The cheesemaker needs to know how to sort it out.

What Wisconsin Cheese Tastes Like

Wisconsin cheese tastes milky, salty, nutty, sweet, crumbly with a hint of crystallization, smooth like sour cream, spicy, pungent, chalky, squeaky, fruity, lip-smackingly buttery, and, overall, delicious. More varieties of cheese are made in Wisconsin than even your average cheesemaker would guess, and more than thirty varieties have a master cheesemaker attached to their names.

There is Wisconsin cheese perfect for a Little Caesar's pizza or a Cheez-It; there is Wisconsin cheese perfect for an after-dinner course at the best-respected restaurants in Manhattan or Tokyo. Masters preside over the making of a good deal of it, and much of the best of it. At the 2008 World Championship Cheese Contest, Wisconsin cheesemakers captured twenty-seven of seventy-seven gold medals. That's more than any other state (New York took five) and more than any other country (the Netherlands had eight medals).

County Highways

In *Travels with Charley*, John Steinbeck wrote about the ongoing expansion of interstate highways in America.

> These great roads are wonderful for moving goods but not for inspection of a countryside. You are bound to the wheel and your eyes to the car ahead and to the rear-view mirror for the car behind and the side mirror for the car or truck about to pass, and at the same time you must read all the signs for fear you may miss some instructions or orders. No roadside stands selling squash juice, no antique stores, no farm products or factory outlets. When we get these thruways across the whole country, as we will and must, it will be possible to drive from New York to California without seeing a single thing.

On the road to visit Wisconsin master cheesemakers, an observant traveler will spot a lot more than cheese and cows (of which there are plenty). You might spot a bald eagle by the side of the road, working on some roadkill before flying off into the distance. You might drive past the world's largest talking cow in Neillsville. You'll almost certainly see the Wisconsin Amish riding in their black buggies and tending to their dairy farms. You'll eat Wisconsin road food: pork chops and potatoes, applewood-smoked bacon, fried walleye, bratwurst, grilled cheese sandwiches, and homemade pie. And you'll be constantly humbled by the quiet hospitality of the people you meet.

Also, there is a lot of Packers memorabilia everywhere.

The Masters

OF GREEN COUNTY

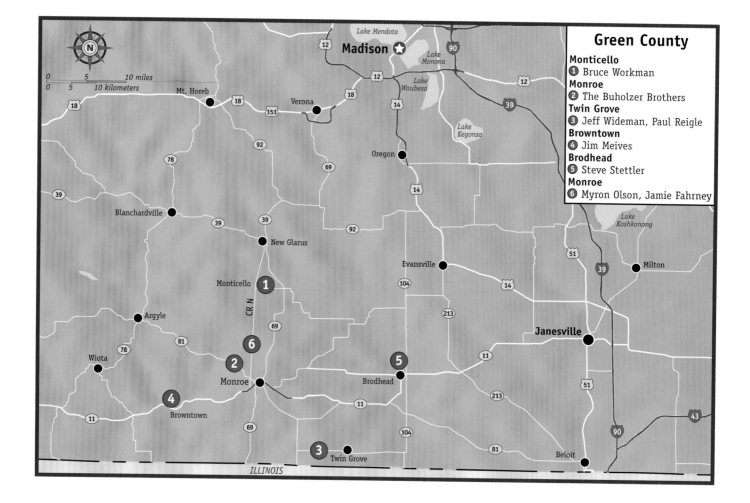

Lake Mendota
Madison
Lake Monona
Lake Waubesa
Lake Kegonsa
Lake Koshkonong

0   5   10 miles
0   5   10 kilometers

Mt. Horeb
Verona
Oregon
Blanchardville
New Glarus
Evansville
Milton
Monticello   1
Argyle
6
Wiota   2   Janesville
5
4   Monroe
Brodhead
Browntown
3 Twin Grove
Beloit

ILLINOIS

IF YOU ORDER THE LIMBURGER SANDWICH at Baumgartner's Cheese Store and Tavern in Monroe, Wisconsin, it soon becomes evident that the tavern isn't fooling around. This isn't a young limburger, still mild and crumbly, nor is it a middle-aged fellow, thickly scented but still acceptable in polite company. The Baumgartner's sandwich comes out smeared with a thick layer of ripe, ancient, almost liquid cheese and raw onions. The onions, used to getting their way in most situations, are beaten into cringing submission by the smell of the cheese, which can tactfully be described as "powerful." A single Andes mint atop the sandwich only plays up the seriousness of the situation.

In 1880 limburger was described by local author John Luchsinger as "a premeditated outrage on the organs of smell," which is tough but fair. Why would anyone choose to eat a cheese that, to some extent, is the gastronomic equivalent of being sprayed in the face by a skunk?

Pride in one's Swiss German heritage is the answer for some, but the truth is, the stuff is actually pretty delicious. It persists in Green County culture not simply because it's a novelty; connoisseurs understand that the rolling cloud of musk emitted from the cheese signals a flavor gold mine. There's a great deal of depth, earthy nuance, and lip-smacking flavor in a piece of limburger, although it pays to select the age of your cheese carefully.

"Limburger cheese . . . you can't have Christmas around here without it," says a clerk at Monroe Madness, a shirt shop that sells "Monroe Cheesemakers" shirts in honor of the local high school team. "You can't go to a party without someone putting it in your face, with onions and crackers."

Baumgartner's is ground zero for Green County Cheese Days, a biennial event that takes place on the third weekend of September in even-numbered years. And while the limburger sandwich is a must for first-time visitors, the selection embraces many milder and more widely loved favorites.

It seems as if cheese is inescapable in Monroe. A visit to Chocolate Temptations, a local coffee shop, in January 2008 led to eavesdropping on a conversation between two women, one in her midforties, the other older. It soon becomes clear that the younger woman is an editor for the Swiss Colony catalog, and her coffee partner is the artist responsible for the catalog's mouse mascot, Chris.

"He's always struggling to do a big job," says the editor. "But couldn't he do a big job *joyfully*?" The artist concedes that he probably could.

The tackling of a big job joyfully describes, in a nutshell, what Green County cheese artisans like Bruce Workman or Jeff Wideman do on a day-to-day basis. For local cheesemakers, the county's Swiss heritage provides a flesh-and-blood link to the product they make on a daily basis.

"We can go back to why the immigrants came to this area in the first place out of Switzerland," says Wideman, a master certified in monterey jack and cheddar cheeses. "It was because of our ground. It's a limestone base here that produces such fine grasses."

Those grasses, in turn, are transformed by the bellies of cows into fine milk, which makes some of the country's best-regarded cheeses.

"The first Swiss immigrants came here in about 1847," says Wideman. "At that time, cheesemaking was just woman's work in the kitchen—they made alpekäse or other Swiss-type cheeses."

A wheat blight changed the way Green County regarded its cheese production, and set it on its way to being a world cheese capital in the 1920s.

"When the chinch bug came through this area, there was no way to control it. It wiped out the wheat industry, and a lot of them reverted to the cheesemaking they had brought with them from Switzerland," says Wideman. "What was once woman's work became the man's job, and they produced more milk and other crops besides wheat so that they had animal feed. And the cheesemaking industry evolved from there."

Bruce Workman used this stencil to label his wheels of swiss.

Cooperative cheese plants became a logical next step for the farmers. At one point, the county had more than two hundred plants, most of which were small three-, four-, or five-farmer operations. Monroe became a major cheese hub.

"I don't know how many cheese buyers there were in Monroe, maybe thirty at least," says Wideman. "They each had six, seven, eight factories they bought cheese from exclusively."

If Wisconsin was the cheese capital of America, so Monroe was (and arguably still is, at least in density of masters) the cheese capital of Wisconsin.

"The hub of the whole cheese industry was Monroe," Wideman says. "And the railroad was very important. The Milwaukee Road and the Illinois Central came through there, and they had two depots, one on the north side of town and one on the south side of town. Along those rail systems were all the cheese warehouses."

While the primacy of Monroe has faded in terms of volume and logistics, Green County still has a tremendous wealth of international award-winning knowledge, as symbolized by the ten master cheesemakers still working within its borders. From Bruce Workman, whose Swiss copper kettle is a shining example of tradition embraced and continued, to the Buholzer family, who have embraced the future of industrial-scale feta manufacturing, the county remains abuzz with craftspeople who are defined by—and help to define—Wisconsin cheese.

The sign and entryway to Baumgartner's Cheese Store and Tavern in Monroe.

Bruce Workman

Edelweiss Creamery, Monticello, Wisconsin
http://www.edelweisscreamery.com/

Master of gruyère, baby swiss, butterkäse, havarti, raclette, emmentaler, and specialty swiss

I wanted to be a culinary chef, and I am. I just use larger vessels.

Bruce Workman feels the curd
to see when the emmentaler is
ready to be poured into forms.

AT FIVE IN THE MORNING, most Americans are asleep. They are snoozing soundly, tucked into a layer cake of warm sheets and blankets in a climate-controlled bedroom. Work—probably at an office—is still safely three to four hours in the future.

At five in the morning on any given weekday, Bruce Workman is, quite possibly, wrestling a milk line six inches in diameter, kinking the hose precisely in order to facilitate the flow of liquid within. Seconds later, he's clambering up to the top of the bulk truck, firing a hose into the truck's interior to flush out the last, valuable bits of milk solids still clinging to the tank. And then, with little warning, he has practically jogged back into the humidity of the Edelweiss Creamery to check on a European-made copper vat containing what will soon be some of Green County's finest swiss cheese. He's massaging a piece of curd to get a sense of where the vat's at; this one is taking a little longer than usual, in terms of hitting the right level of acidity.

A number of Wisconsin cheesemakers literally throw their backs into their work, but Workman—the current holder of the most master cheesemaker certifications—is among the most dynamic. He argues that hands-on work is the *x* factor that sets his product apart.

"It's open-vat, hands-on cheesemaking, with a cheesemaker who takes the time to know what's going on with the vats from start to finish." he says. "If you look downstairs, there are two of us who are running the vats, so we always know what's going on."

Workman has friends who work at big plants, and he doesn't run down their efforts; but, still, the old-school open-vat methods are how he'd prefer to do business. "In an enclosed vat environment, you're at the whim of the computer," he says. "Milk is such a fragile and complex thing. . . . If you don't keep an eye on it, physically, you don't know what you have. I mean, you saw the swiss downstairs. It was not ready to cut. If I had left that in a closed vat, the vat would've said, 'Ah, guess what, it's time to go,' and we're on our way."

Dawn breaks at Edelweiss Creamery. By 10 a.m. Bruce Workman has already put in a full workday.

The co-op at Edelweiss represents a considerable personal gamble for Workman. In order to do the kind of soulful cheesemaking he most enjoys, he bought up an old plant that was far from operational. "Everybody said I was an idiot," he says with a laugh. "The building was a wreck—the ceilings had collapsed and the floors had buckled." He spent six months working to gut and refurbish the place, which now employs six people. "The tile walls and windows are the only original parts of the plant," he says.

Bruce Workman climbs atop a bulk truck to wash out the last of the milk from the tank.

The advantage of building the plant his way was the ability to fit it out in a manner suited to his product, emmentaler.

"I'm the only one in the U.S. who makes that traditional, real swiss cheese," he says. "We use the press, you see; I bought that in Switzerland. We use the copper kettle; I bought that in Switzerland. That actually came out of the master cheesemakers school. To think of all the cheesemakers who were trained on that. . . . That's pretty cool." The copper kettle itself is a beautiful piece of hardware, like a titan-sized stand mixer with two paddles that make a circular dance through the milk.

Workman boils down the historical significance of his plant: "There used to be over two hundred little cheese plants in this county, all producing authentic copper-kettle swiss. Over the years, as cheesemaking became industrialized and companies worked to reduce their labor costs, it was abandoned. I set out to bring it back."

When he told Felix Roth, one of his former employers at Roth Käse, in New Glarus, that he was planning to quit and start a new plant, Roth did something typical of cheesemakers parting ways: he wished Workman luck and helped his outgoing employee start up.

"'I want to make swiss cheese,' I said to Roth, 'but I don't want to make it one kettle at a time, I can't afford to do that,' and he goes, 'Oh, let me see what I can do,' and I said, 'I know there's equipment in Switzerland,'

and he says, 'Yeah, yeah, some things are coming up, these factories are closing.' The very next day he calls me from Switzerland and says, 'Ah! I found your equipment,' and I'm sayin', 'Ah, you're a little quick. I haven't bought the building yet!'"

Roth let it slide for the time being, but three weeks later he phoned Workman to say that the equipment at the master cheesemakers school was available for a song. "I mean it cost me more to ship it over here than it did to buy it," Workman says.

These forms, imported from Europe, are slowly filled with emmentaler curd.

Workman's business arrangements at Edelweiss hearken back to the old co-op ideal that has been on the ropes in many parts of the state. "We are the first one to come back and start a new co-op in the state of Wisconsin," he says. "The farmers own the building. They own the wastewater field, they own the well, that kind of stuff. I own the equipment and they hire me to make cheese. I get a percentage of the gross. By doing that, there's more return for the farmers," he says. "Now, flipside is—they have to maintain the building. But any equipment issues, those are mine."

The three farmers Workman deals with own about 350 cows, which live in a pasture-fed, more traditional manner than cows raised on a factory farm. The farmers aren't, however, certified organic.

"They don't want to have the headaches of being organic," he says. "Their cows are much healthier, though. Everyone thinks of organic as being these huge, healthy cows but if you walk around, look at organic farms, most of those cows are put in barns.

"But if I look at my pastured cows, they're really healthy," says Workman. "They're getting their exercise twice a day, walking out and walking back. Life expectancy of the pastured cow that's out there, you're lookin' at thirteen–fifteen years! Cow that slept in a barn, standing on the cement, doesn't get much exercise—five–seven years. It's hard on their legs. It's hard on their hoofs."

Workman, of course, is no hypocrite on the exercise front; his punishing daily schedule has left him extraordinarily fit, if somewhat tired during normal daylight hours. In order to save money, Workman works a 10 p.m. to 10 a.m. schedule to take advantage of off-peak electricity rates. He isn't busy seven days a week, however; on the weekend, he sleeps in until 4 a.m.

In a brief moment of calm, Bruce Workman explains the process of refurbishing an old factory.

The Buholzer Brothers:
Ron, Steve, and Dave

Klondike Cheese Company, Monroe, Wisconsin
http://www.klondikecheese.com/

Masters of feta (Ron, Steve, and Dave), brick (Ron), and muenster (Steve and Dave)

Way back, we made a lot of mistakes—and we learned a lot from them.
—STEVE BUHOLZER

DOWN IN GREEN COUNTY, once home almost exclusively to small makers of mostly Swiss- and German-style cheeses, the specialty cheese revolution has wrought strange changes. Once-small factories have mushroomed as others have been converted to homes or demolished. Cheeses from Mediterranean countries have elbowed their way into the mix, providing new outlets for old wellsprings of cheesemaking talent.

At the Klondike Cheese Company, the three Buholzer brothers—all certified master cheesemakers of Swiss heritage—have become makers of feta cheese that embodies the word "quantity" without losing sight of the quality that Green County cheesemakers are known for.

Ron, Dave, and Steve all tackle different parts of the job at their plant, which employs about sixty people. Ron rides herd on maintenance and sales. Dave buys the ingredients and supplies and runs the production schedule. Steve deals with the milk, farmers, and cheesemakers.

After hours, the Buholzer brothers work on cars in a garage behind the plant.

25

Cows dot the winter landscape outside of Brodhead on County Road F.

"Cheesemaking is like driving up the road," says Steve, the youngest brother. "You try to stay near the center line. With three opinions, it's a lot easier to figure out how to keep from weaving too far in either direction. The three of us could always talk," he adds. "We try to do that now with the next generation. Hopefully we can pass along what little knowledge we have here."

The plant is one of the few in Wisconsin that is truly multigenerational, with a third generation rising through the ranks. In addition to the three brothers (who were schooled in cheesemaking by their father, Alvin), Steve's daughter, Melissa Erdley, and her husband, Matt, have a hand in the business, as do Ron's sons, Luke and Matt, and Steve's son, Adam, and his wife, Teena.

"This started out as a small plant," says Ron, the eldest brother. "We were all on the floor. The actual business end of it and stuff, well, our dad did it. And then as we got bigger, things just evolved. One person just couldn't take care of it all anymore."

A machine called the coagulator dominates the Klondike Cheese Company's feta-making process. If fellow Green County cheesemaker Bruce Workman is the John Henry of the cheesemaking business, than surely the coagulator is the steam-powered hammer.

TASTING NOTES: KLONDIKE FETA

Feta can sometimes be overly astringent and hide more subtle flavors beneath an acidic wash of taste, but this feta maintains a tangy flavor without overpowering the cheese base. It has a nice lemon aftertaste, and is firm and chalky in texture but easy to crumble.

Imagine a half-cylindrical tank several feet in diameter that stretches for more than a hundred feet. Every few feet, a massive, semicircular steel plate marks off a cell that will hold close to a ton of milk. The whole thing is propelled, in slow motion, by a circular belt. Pasteurized milk is pumped into cells; as the milk moves through the cells, rennet separates the milk into whey and curd. At the far end of the tank, rotating knives and a wire cutter that jerks back and forth hew a gridlike pattern into the sheets of curd.

On a big day, Klondike will produce ninety thousand or more pounds of feta cheese. Most is destined for food service, although about 20 percent is sold at retail under the Odyssey brand. Klondike also produces muenster, brick, and havarti, but feta is the keystone of the business.

Despite the might of the machine, a great deal of human thought and old-fashioned tinkering are key to maintaining the plant's award-winning quality. The feta that comes out of Klondike earned first place awards in 2006 from the World Championship Cheese Contest, the American Cheese Society, and the Wisconsin State Fair.

"With feta being highly acidified, it is a challenge to get your cultures to go right where you want them and keep them in a tight range," says Steve. "Because of the process, instead of taking four hours to make a piece of muenster cheese, for example, it actually takes fifteen–sixteen hours, in order for the cheese to come out. A little variability in your culture, because it is working so long in your cheese, makes a big difference. Per se the mechanics are extremely simple, but in reality it is very difficult to make consistently—there's not a lot of steps in the process."

Feta, as made by the Buholzers of Klondike Cheese Company.

Although the Buholzers buy culture from starter houses, they mix their own blend.

"That is part of the reason we were able to get into feta cheese—we have a lot of starter culture experience and we always grow our own," says Steve.

The result? A cheese that's tangy, smooth, not harsh, not bitter, "salty but not too salty." "It is not supposed to be bitter, it is supposed to be tangy and have that lipase taste to it," adds Ron. "It is a salty cheese, but not overpowering."

Havarti cheese, pressed under whey, at Klondike Cheese Company.

Achieving a good feta is a matter of working closely with the microfauna that shape the cheese's flavor profile. That, in turn, requires constant innovation.

"There is a naturally occurring thing called bacteriophage that is Mother Nature's protective organism," says Ron. "It basically tries to kill your starter culture. You can't just use one starter culture over and over and over again, and you have to constantly be rotating. That brings a lot of the challenge. If you could just find yourself a culture and go with it, that would be way too easy."

The challenge of cheesemaking was part of what drove the brothers to the masters program. "I took one course that had to do with flavors, and adding flavors and creating flavors," says Dave. "It was kind of one of these 'wow' things. You learn how flavors work. How your senses work, really."

The courses taken to be certified as master cheesemakers were critical, according to Dave, to understanding the inner workings of cheese. "We don't have very much college education," he says. "You know if you do this, then this happens, and you take the course and find out why. This is *why* this happens. Gaining that knowledge, now I know if I do this *and* do this, I should get this result.

"I guess probably I got the biggest bang out of that part of it," he adds. "Not that I understand completely all of it but I know quite a bit more about it."

Ask the Buholzer boys what they do for fun and you're likely to be met by a trio of impish grins. Famous (or infamous) among their colleagues, the Buholzers play as hard as they work, rebuilding and driving—not racing, they insist—souped-up cars at various tracks and rallies.

A professional-sized garage dominates one of the plant's outbuildings, filled with cars in various states. The guys visibly relax when they cross the threshold. This isn't just a garage—it's a clubhouse. A sign high on the wall reads: "Life is not a journey to the grave with the intention of arriving safely in a pretty and well-preserved body, but rather to skid in broadside, thoroughly used up, totally worn out, and loudly proclaiming—Wow! What a ride."

Without seeing the guys take their cars out for a spin, it's difficult to say exactly how literally the sign should be interpreted. But it seems safe to say it's somewhere between a motto and a personal mantra for the three still-rambunctious brothers.

"A lot of stuff we do together, because we work together, but we also enjoy each other's company," says Dave. "I guess it is kind of highly unusual for three siblings to get along that well. If there's a problem, we can sit down and work it out. There are no rivalries, no ideas about 'I am working harder than he is,' or whatever. We all take our time off as we can, and work when we need to. And that is pretty much the way it has always been."

Jeff Wideman and Paul Reigle

<small>Maple Leaf Cheese</small>, Monroe, Wisconsin
http://www.mapleleafcheese.com/

Masters of monterey jack and cheddar (Wideman), yogurt cheese (Reigle)

There's not an "I" in this business. It's about everybody from the farmer to the milk hauler to the people in the plant—everybody's a part of that award.

—JEFF WIDEMAN

Jeff Wideman explains the
history of Maple Leaf Cheese.

IT'S HARD TO GENERALIZE about cheesemakers, but one rule of thumb generally seems to hold true: the smaller the plant, the more hats the cheesemaker wears.

Paul Reigle, one of two master cheesemakers at Maple Leaf Cheese, sums up his early, frantic days at the plant with a mixture of pride and head-shaking wonder. "[In the 1980s] we didn't have a maintenance man, so we did everything—piping, electrical, cheesemaking . . ."

The cooperative's other master, Jeff Wideman, picks up where Paul trails off. "Boiler teardowns. . . . We'd take the boiler apart ourselves every three months," he says. "Pipe . . . all that pipe. . . . We piped miles of pipe. We had our own trucks at that time that were hauling milk and hauling whey that we had to deal with. We used to be making cheese until late in the morning," he adds. "At noon we'd have lunch, and then we had projects in that old building to no end. We piped and piped and piped. A lot of times it'd be five or six o'clock when we'd get done."

"Ten-minute project, figure . . . maybe an hour," says Reigle.

Wideman and Reigle got their start at the plant in the early '80s, and faced far more than a bunch of urgent building improvements; they faced a business plan that was out of date and destined to doom the plant.

"We made monterey jack through the winter, forty-pound blocks, and rindless block swiss in the summertime when there was grass milk available," recalls Wideman. "For a small plant to survive making rindless block and monterey jack block, that wasn't going to happen. Both are considered commodity items, in this day and age especially."

A WISCONSIN CHEESE HISTORY TIMELINE

1858 Wisconsin's first commercial cheese factory established in Sheboygan Falls

1872 Wisconsin Dairymen's Association founded in Watertown

1873 Reduced freight rates and first shipment of Wisconsin cheese to eastern markets by refrigerator car effected by dairy pioneer W. D. Hoard

1879 Predecessor to the Wisconsin Cheese Exchange set up in Plymouth

1885 National magazine edition of *Hoard's Dairyman* launched; colby cheese invented near Colby, Wisconsin

1890 Nation's first dairy school established at the University of Wisconsin; Babcock Test for measuring butterfat in milk developed at the UW

1918 Wisconsin Cheese Exchange (later renamed the National Cheese Exchange) established in Plymouth

1921 Nation's first grading of cheese for quality instituted in Wisconsin

1933 Cold-pack method of producing cheese spread perfected in Kaukauna

1940 U.S. declared free from tuberculosis in cattle, the successful culmination of campaign started by W. D. Hoard forty-five years earlier

1974 National Cheese Exchange founded in Green Bay

1976 Walter V. Price Cheese Research Institute organized by Norm Olson

1983 Mandatory state milk marketing order approved by milk producers, leading to creation of Wisconsin Milk Marketing Board

1986 Funding for Center for Dairy Research, which grows in the next twenty years from three staffers to more than thirty, secured by Norm Olson

1994 First class of candidates in Wisconsin Master Cheesemaker Program

1997 National Cheese Exchange replaced by Chicago Mercantile Exchange; graduation of first class of master cheesemakers

2008 Fiftieth certified Wisconsin master cheesemaker, Tom Torkelson, graduates from the program

Sources: Wisconsin Milk Marketing Board; *Hoard's Dairyman*; *Wisconsin's Past and Present*

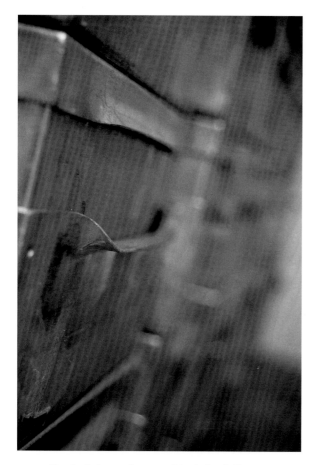

Stacked cheese forms at Maple Leaf Cheese.

Wideman had different ideas for the little plant. "We bought our first specialty forms in 1982, and we still are using some of those today," he says. "A lot of the twelve-pound deli wheel forms we got out of Holland. And I remember one of the older gentlemen I was working with looking at them and saying, 'Boy, I didn't think we were going to get into this this big.' He was great, but he was getting older, and he just couldn't see what was coming."

Physical plant and business challenges are one thing; the cheese itself poses its own set of complications. "First of all, you're working with a live product," says Reigle. "That vat may not work like this vat. You've got to kind of know how to adjust for it. It's not an assembly line; you can't go by the clock. Everything works a little different. You never know when a breakdown's going to happen."

"That's when you really have to shine," adds Wideman. "Years ago, you might have some wild milk some days, and then you'd better dig into your bag of tricks. It's not cookie cutter."

Wild milk is less common in the modern era of standardized production; once upon a time, it drove even master makers crazy on a regular basis.

"You know, a farmer, not intentionally, might have a cooler problem," says Wideman. "Then all of a sudden, when that milk's been in the heat, it's—oh, wow, we've got something different here today. Maybe you notice with all your senses you use in making cheese—your nose, maybe the color of the whey is a little different, oh, jeez, something's not right here today. That vat's a little slow, or that kettle isn't stirring out as quick as you think it should. You need to be ready to adjust."

That willingness to adjust applies equally to the business aspect of cheesemaking. Wideman, an experienced cheese marketer as well as maker, says he's seen some radical changes over the years in terms of how cheese is sold.

"The true co-ops, here in the area—as I mentioned before, Monroe was the hub of the cheese industry and a true co-op. You took the milk in, you never owned the milk, the farmers gave you the milk to make into a marketable product—you had one buyer who took everything you made," he says. "The milk came in, you made cheese, you set up a truck to pick it up, you might've graded it at the factory or shipped it into storage and graded it there, and there was a check transferred from the buyer to your operating bank where your co-op's account was, and you got a percentage of that, and it was all done. You never saw the check.

"But that all changed," Wideman says, "when we got into the specialty business. I remember my first customer was in Lancaster, Pennsylvania, in March of 1981. It was the first time Maple Leaf had ever sold a pound of cheese outside of Monroe. That was a big deal. The guy called us up, he was looking for this, but we showed him that, he got interested in that, and we kept doing business. To this day, we still do business with that customer. Actually second generation there. The industry was changing. People began to realize they could come directly to the plant. And there were a lot of problems with that in the community."

Near Maple Leaf Cheese in Twin Grove, Wisconsin.

That new responsiveness to the market—and the fading of old habits of selling and making—explains one of Maple Leaf's more unusual products, the yogurt cheese for which Reigle received his master's certification.

"It's a lightly colored, open-bodied lactose-free lower sodium type cheese," Reigle says. "It's attractive to the people who are lactose intolerant."

Wideman, sotto voce, prompts Reigle: "Acidophilus bifidus . . ."

"I can hardly say those words," says Reigle, grinning. But he knows his cheese; when asked how he produces a lactose-free cheese, he responds, "That's pretty much all done by the starters we use. It's done by the yogurt culture. It'll consume the lactose."

Paul Reigle and Jeff Wideman stand outside Maple Leaf Cheese in Green County.

"The right answer here is you're supposed to tell 'em: 'That's why I'm a master cheesemaker,'" Wideman adds with a laugh.

Like many of Wisconsin's more unusual specialty cheeses, Maple Leaf's yogurt cheese originated with a customer request.

"We met some people from out East," says Wideman. "They came to us and wanted to know if we could develop a yogurt cheese for them, using acidophilus bifidus probiotic cultures, for the health benefits, low in sodium."

Not surprisingly, the Center for Dairy Research played a key role in developing the cheese. "John Jaeggi and his staff—you know, I saw John Jaeggi get on the school bus for the first time," recalls Wideman. "We have very close ties, because of the way we grew up here in this little village. So we worked on this project, and it took us about two years to develop that cheese. And of course, Paul was involved with that all the way through. It started out, nine or ten years ago at this point."

A pitch from Jim Path at the CDR planted the seed that led to both of Maple Leaf's masters getting their medals.

"Oh, jeez," says Wideman. "Going back to school and going to the classes and going up to Babcock Hall and the CDR department—it was just great. You get to go in and play with all that equipment, and do things you just don't have the time or equipment to do on site, for the most part. And if you think you know this business, you'd better get out, because . . . it never quits."

"You get to meet more people," adds Reigle. "I guess on that part of it, I've only worked in one cheese plant. So I'd never really had the chance to talk to a lot of people in other plants. This gave me a chance to talk to other people and see what they're doing."

The program was as challenging, says Wideman, as it was rewarding. "I was forty-eight or forty-nine years old when I went back to school," he says. "And that's not easy. And writing that test was . . . Jeez, I don't know how many hours it took me to write that test. When I wrote that test I'd wake up at four in the morning and write until seven or seven thirty, then come to the plant."

And although the test was plenty challenging, Wideman remembers the entrance interview as being the roughest part of the experience. "Mike Dean— he's now passed away—interviewed me when I entered the program, and some of the other peers, so to speak, they'll pick you apart," he says. "They'll tell you, 'You're very strong in this area, but you're extremely weak in this area.' And maybe you didn't realize that. 'And this is what we need you to work on.'

"It's a bit humbling," Wideman adds. "If you're not open to that, you better not be in the program."

Paul Reigle shows off the curd for his plant's yogurt cheese.

Jim Meives

Chula Vista Cheese Company, Browntown, Wisconsin
http://www.1-888-vvsupremo.com/

Master of queso blanco and brick

*I love 'em all, from brie to colby to aged cheddar, and I cannot pick out a favorite cheese.
I mean, try to do that, you know?*

GEARED FOR ACADEMIA BY A UNIVERSITY PROFESSOR FATHER, Jim Meives surprised everyone—including himself—by extending a college hiatus into a full-blown career.

"I told my father I was gonna be a cheesemaker and he hit the roof. 'You're gonna do what?!' But I just loved it," Meives recalls. "As it turned out, I excelled at cheesemaking. And," he says, "I met my wife in the packing room."

For a young cheesemaker taking stock of his industry, the experience was a formative one. The small plant did a little of everything, making roughly forty varieties of cheese. More importantly, it employed Wisconsin cheese legend Willi Lehner Sr.

TASTING NOTES: CHIHUAHUA

Queso blanco is usually described generically as a Hispanic melting cheese, and the Chihuahua brand has been created exactly to fit this description. It tastes like a mix between a young cheddar and a mozzarella, combining the mild acidic flavor of cheddar with a soft, smooth texture. It grates and melts superbly without crumbling and works well as a breakfast cheese—try roasting potatoes with rosemary and topping with shredded Chihuahua and a fried egg.

"So I developed a friendship, a relationship, with a man who is now my father-in-law," Meives says. "He ran the plant, and was my mentor. We hit it off, and we worked well together. His daughter Mary Lehner was in Switzerland, and she came back, and she started working at the cheese plant, and I fell in love with her and we got married and lived happily ever after," he says with a laugh.

Circumstances eventually led to Meives's setting up his own shop, Chula Vista Cheese Company, in partnership with Willi Lehner Sr. and a cheese marketing firm called V&V Supremo. There, he began production of a special type of queso blanco. "[V&V] wanted to streamline their Chihuahua cheese," he says. "It's a Hispanic melting cheese, with a unique flavor profile that we developed, and they wanted it to come from one source. It was just a perfect marriage."

Pressed to describe the flavor of his signature cheese, Meives falters a bit—like many cheeses, it's tough to nail down with total precision. "If I were to . . . man," he says. "Well, it'd be between a muenster and a colby. You can put it in between, but it's got its own unique profile."

Meives makes about forty thousand pounds of Chihuahua a day, no mean feat for a small plant making a cheese for a specialized market. But as the Hispanic population booms—along with a national love affair with south-of-the-border cooking—Meives has found himself in a good market position.

"Nobody's immune to competition," he adds. "We've had a relative wave of Hispanic cheese but we were the front-runner for a long time. At one time we were one of the only ones out there. And now a lot of people are on the bandwagon. But our market is good. I'm optimistic."

Jim Meives stands outside his Green County plant on a cold January morning.

Part of that optimism is derived from the knowledge taken from the master cheesemaker's course. Meives went in, he says, overconfident—and emerged a more fully rounded cheesemaker. "I honestly went into the cheesemaker's short course thinking I'd be teaching it, and I learned a lot," he says. "And that was kinda humbling, you know?"

At the end of the process, however, there's a sense of accomplishment, he says. "You get that medal—and we're aware, like I say, we're a little more aware of each step that we're doing."

When Meives is asked if he has a favorite recipe involving his cheese, there's not even a second's hesitation. "I make the best jalapeño bean dip in the *world*!" he proclaims.

A single cow in a field along Highway 69 near Belleville.

Steve Stettler

Decatur Dairy, Brodhead, Wisconsin
http://www.decaturdairy.com/

Master of havarti, muenster, brick, and farmer

*I was nineteen years old when my dad offered me part of the company. And there are
very few guys who get a chance to buy into a company at the age of nineteen.*

THERE'S A TENDENCY WHEN TALKING TO OUTSIDERS—journalists,
authors, other laypeople—to put a pretty face on the Wisconsin dairy
industry. It's good marketing, and someone's got to sing its praises.
Master cheesemaker Steve Stettler, however, isn't one to shy away from
straight talk.

"It's a tough business," Stettler says. "The small cheese factories, it's
going to be tough. The market right now is extremely high. You have
all the day traders, this thing with the milk futures and all that are
impacting our pricing. It's not only hard on the cheesemaker, it's hard
on the people in sales, and your buyers. That whole market right now is
not very stable."

Stettler looks at a market with good cheese sales and sees the other
side of things: feed prices are high, fuel prices are high, and the amount
of gyration has increased dramatically in recent years.

"The instability is a tough thing right now," Stettler says. "I've made
cheese for over thirty years. It used to be if the market moved three
cents, it was a huge deal. And now it moves a dime."

Stettler is constantly keeping up with new trends that sweep the
industry. Growth hormone–free milk may be one of the future profit
centers for cheesemaking, Stettler suggests. "Right now, all the fluid

Steve Stettler, inside Decatur Dairy
in Green County.

39

milk is tending to go rBGH free," he says. "So I see a huge demand in the cheese market for product that is rBGH free. But do you get in right away, or do you wait?"

Stettler is a hands-on cheesemaker ("I'm not an office guy, let's go with that," he says when asked about which side of the business he enjoys), and he's built up his business by making award-winning cheese and fighting to make sure his people stay connected to the product.

"I didn't go full automation—because I always want them to be stickin' their hands in it—so I don't have automatic cutters," he says. "We check the cut and do that by hand, instead of just relying on timers. I still want the cheesemaking aspect of adding ingredients and checking the curd. If your milk has a different acid, your vats will react a little different. Even before we pump it, we stick our hands in to feel the curd and make sure it is what it's supposed to be."

Stettler's been cheesemaker and co-op manager for the Decatur Dairy factory since 1982, and he's dealt with a lot of issues other than the quality of the cheese being shipped from his plant. In a world of leveraged buyouts, multinational corporations, and hedge funds, the phrase "dairy co-op" has an almost charming ring to it. But co-ops are businesses, too; they're not magically conflict free.

Corn that has stayed on the stalk along County Road D between Madison and Belleville.

"About a year ago this time, they were trying to fire me," Stettler says of his co-op board. "It's a complicated issue. The old board was led to believe I wasn't returning all the money they were entitled to. And the majority of the farmers were happy with what they were getting, because it was more than they'd get anywhere else. The bottom line was we all spent a lot of money to find out that they probably owed me some money."

On top of making cheese, wrestling with the ins and outs of being part of a co-op, and dealing with sales, Stettler also tries to stay at the top of cheesemaking's steep learning curve. When he went into making havarti, he studied with makers in Europe to get an Old World perspective on the cheese.

"I was kind of amazed—they were really friendly and opened their doors up," Stettler says. "The little cheese plants would show me what kind of cultures to use, if I could get 'em here. Some cultures weren't available at that time, but they are now."

Stettler also spent time in a Danish cheesemaking school, where the scope and quality of the education made a big impression upon him. "They do everything there—restaurants, cheese, baking—but they have a huge dairy section," he says. "It's actually superior to what UW has. They're into UF-ing [ultrafiltration] and RO-ing [reverse osmosis]—they're into all that stuff there. So when you leave there, you pretty much have touched on everything about cheesemaking."

When he's not making cheese, Stettler tours the open road on a motorcycle. "I'm not a racer," he says. "I'm just a guy who goes out with a bunch of boys . . . and do a little bikin'. We went to Europe last year for two weeks with nine guys. We flew into Frankfurt, and then we just took off. We went to Austria. We went to Italy, and then to Switzerland. We spent about nine days in Switzerland. We went to a bunch of different cheese factories. And then we went back into Germany for a couple days. That was a good trip."

Steve Stettler. (courtesy of Wisconsin Milk Marketing Board)

Myron Olson and Jamie Fahrney

CHALET CHEESE COOPERATIVE, Monroe, Wisconsin
phone (608) 325-4343

Masters of baby swiss and brick (Olson and Fahrney), limburger (Olson)

When you say limburger, right away your connotation is: 'Oh, it is nasty.'
I have seen all the jokes. I have heard all the things.
—MYRON OLSON

Myron Olson shows off some of
Chalet's limburger cheese.

UNLIKE SOME OF THE BIGGER GUNS in a cheesemaker's arsenal—stainless steel rakes and shovels, wire screens and machetelike curd knives—a cheese trier feels like a precision instrument. Made from surgical steel and clocking in at about nine inches long, the trier looks like a shiny letter T—the top of the letter is a satisfyingly heavy handle that you can wrap a fist around, while the bottom consists of a hollow cylinder, cut in half to form a trough or U shape.

If you're visiting Chalet Cheese Cooperative in Green Country, Wisconsin, and cheesemaker Myron Olson is feeling expansive, he'll take you in to where the plant's swiss is cooled in wooden boxes. Each box can be opened for sampling, and Olson can—and will—insert a trier, turn it 180 degrees, and withdraw a plug of still-warm cheese.

The taste is shockingly pleasant—intensely delicate, sweet, mellow, buttery, and touched by just a bit of swiss cheese tang. It helps that the cheese is warm, but the real key lies in the make. For starters, Chalet uses whole milk in its cheeses.

"We leave all the fat in it, so it tends to give a smoother mouth feel, a little more smacking of the lips," Olson says. "When you're done with it you want to go back and have another piece. When you make a piece of cheese that does that, then you know you have made it."

Fellow master cheesemaker and colleague Jamie Fahrney takes the lead on swiss. "The eye formation—that's the toughest thing," he says. "It's determined by the cooking of the cheese, the pressing, how long it's left in the warm room—there are so many things, I could go on forever about it. For me, it was a challenge."

Chalet swiss also has less moisture than many competitors—it's about 39 percent, even though it could be up to 43 percent. More moisture means more money, but Olson would rather have a cheese that ages well. Too much water can lead to an ammonia smell on the back end of its lifecycle.

But although the company's swiss is the mainstay of its business, Chalet and Olson have developed an outsized international reputation for another cheese: limburger. The butt of endless jokes, a regular supporting player on animated comedies from the 1940s and '50s, and a cheese long regarded as something eaten only by country uncles, limburger is still going strong at Chalet, the last maker of the cheese in the Americas.

Although limburger represents only 20 percent of the company's production, it takes up half the plant's workforce. "Lot of hand

A fence disappears into the winter landscape outside of Brodhead.

Myron Olson and Jamie Fahrney of Chalet Cheese Cooperative in Monroe hold a board full of limburger cheese. They are the only makers of limburger in the country. (courtesy of Wisconsin Milk Marketing Board)

labor involved with it," Olson says. "You have to salt the cheese by hand, you have to smear the cheese [with a bacteria-boosting wash] by hand, and then the wrapping is done by hand, the weighing out is done by hand, labeling is done by hand."

Machines can't deal with limburger, which is a sticky, fussy cheese to handle; a team of hard-working Green Country residents, however, seem to find it a breeze, packing it, wrapping it, labeling it, and chatting among themselves in one of the plant's back rooms.

Why hassle with such a fussy, ill-regarded cheese?

Limburger is deceptively delicious, and surprisingly complicated. In its early stages of development (one to two months of age) it actually resembles a feta—a bright flavor, and a crumbly texture. At three to four months of age, it resembles a strong brie or camembert—an earthy flavor, a softer and more buttery texture, and a powerful, but not overwhelming, odor. Only at five to six months does the cheese give off the plumes of ammoniated stink that make it so notorious. But even then, it's a brilliant culinary power forward, when teamed up with ingredients (rye bread, raw red onions, strong mustard) that are its equal. Like most smear-ripened cheese, the smell is far stronger (and infinitely more obnoxious) than the rich, complicated flavor. But public prejudice against limburger is longstanding and deeply felt.

"A few years ago we had a chef in Chicago and she loved limburger," says Olson. "So she put 'Limburger and Dumplings' on her menu. Couldn't sell anything. Next week—same people, same restaurant—she put it back on her menu as 'Smear Ripened Cheese and Dumplings.' People went wild for it."

This isn't surprising—smear-ripened cheese has been booming recently.

"What I find interesting, the last ten years has been this move back to the stinky cheese," says Olson. "You have these

Myron Olson explains that the limburger made in his plant thrives on the wooden boards that have been inoculated with the correct bacteria.

artisans and are they going to make a bandaged cheddar or are they going to make a fresh mozzarella? A lot of them have gone to the smear cheese, the washed rind cheese. Because people like it."

What people don't like is the reigning image of limburger—a cheese so pungent that it needs to be stored in a Mason jar. On the porch.

"But if you give it a fancy French name and give the person a taste, there is a chance they'll eat it," he says. "When they eat it, probably half the time they are like: 'That's not too bad. That actually tastes pretty good.' But when you take the same person and say, 'Here is a piece of limburger,' . . . 'Oh, no way, I'm not going to eat it.'"

Packaging stamps at Chalet speak to the variety of cheeses made at the plant.

There's nothing stopping Olson from developing a new version of limburger with a fresh name, or repackaging and relabeling the old German country favorite. But he won't have it.

"Why don't I just let the artisans and the others make their taleggios and the smear cheese," he says. "I'll make limburger, just leave my limburger alone. If somebody else comes in and says, 'I'm gonna make limburger,' we will have a battle. Just let me have my limburger and I won't touch your others."

Olson credits his plant—and the old, sometimes decades-old, pine boards on which he ages his cheese—for some of the unique character of his product. In June 2007 the University of Wisconsin took five different pieces of cheese to five different plants, and had each piece of cheese smeared by the resident cheesemaker.

"Each of us took it, smeared it how we thought the smear should be on it, and two months later you had five different pieces of cheeses," says Olson. "Each one's cellar was different, the way they handled it was different, the flavors were different."

Different is actually an understatement, Olson says.

"There were a couple where the flavor came really intense real fast, but with a bigger piece of cheese if you get it too intense the outside will be too far ahead of the center," he adds. "You have to have a nice breakdown. With two of them the smear got ahead of the cheese, so it didn't make as nice a piece of cheese. One was kind of lacking in flavor, and two were what people like, and people did like ours the best out of the five. It was a real interesting experiment."

Olson claims—half-jokingly, although he makes a strong case—that he is, in fact, the most senior of all the master cheesemakers enrolled in the program, despite having graduated in the fourth class. In 1971 Olson got his limburger license from the State of Wisconsin. Because limburger could be made in the late fall with the dregs of the milk and stored until spring, there was an annual flood of cheap limburger on the market, which hurt real makers of the cheese. So the state required special limburger licenses.

"You had to be an apprentice with an actual limburger factory, and then write your limburger license, and at that point they called it a master cheesemaker's license," says Olson. "So actually the limburger makers were the beginning of the master cheesemakers. Otherwise the rest are all general cheesemakers."

You might think that a guy who was a master cheesemaker a quarter century before the program got rolling might be a good teacher; Olson's junior colleague certainly thinks so.

"I enjoy Myron," says Fahrney. "He's taught me a lot—not just about the cheese, but about life in general. He's a good guy. He's taught me everything I know about cheesemaking, too."

The Masters

OF SOUTHWESTERN WISCONSIN

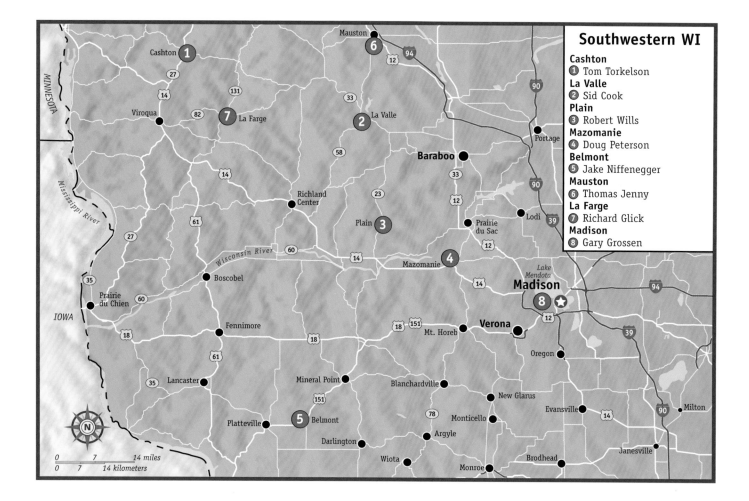

MINNESOTA

Cashton 1

Viroqua

7 La Farge

La Valle 2

Mauston 6

Baraboo

Portage

Mississippi River

Richland Center

Plain 3

Prairie du Sac

Lodi

Wisconsin River

Boscobel

Mazomanie 4

Lake Mendota

Madison 8

IOWA

Prairie du Chien

Fennimore

Mt. Horeb

Verona

Oregon

Lancaster

Mineral Point

Blanchardville

New Glarus

Evansville

Milton

Platteville

5 Belmont

Monticello

Darlington

Argyle

Brodhead

Janesville

Wiota

Monroe

N

0   7   14 miles
0   7   14 kilometers

MADISON IS THE CAPITAL OF THE STATE, and in some ways it's the capital of the state's dairy industry as well. The University of Wisconsin's dairy short course and the Center for Dairy Research are incubators for new talent and wellsprings of old knowledge. The Wisconsin Milk Marketing Board operates from a comfortable office complex in the suburbs of the city. Cheese contests—including the biennial World Championship Cheese Contest—help proclaim up-and-coming makers and confirm veteran masters. And the state legislature presides over the reams of health, safety, and commercial regulations that govern cheesemaking in Wisconsin, protecting consumers and irritating cheesemakers who often need dedicated employees simply to plow through the legal paperwork.

And, more than anything else, Madison mirrors the way the identity of Wisconsin cheese has shifted from commodity blocks of tasteless colby to an increasingly artisan product. Cheesemakers tout their fanciest cheeses at the weekly farmer's market, one of the nation's biggest and best. Fromagination, a cheese store downtown on Capitol Square, shows off some of the state's tastiest and most unusual cheeses side by side with European imports; labels name the dairy and cheesemaker, and clerks are thoroughly briefed on their wares. And at the Old Fashioned, a reinvented Wisconsin supper club on the opposite side of the Square, the menu reflects the land and craftsmanship of the state as a whole. Cheeses from makers such as Uplands Cheese Company, Carr Valley Cheese Company, and Bleu Mont Dairy mingle on cheese plates that could easily stand among the world's best.

The Old Fashioned also offers cheeses from the state's Driftless Area, which includes much of southwestern Wisconsin. It's up there with Door County in terms of sheer beauty, but minus the tourists. Named for the lack of glacial drift (random silt, clay, sand, gravel, and boulders deposited by retreating glaciers), it's a genuinely rustic landscape. Here, the land swells and dips, revealing panoramas of trees, ridges, outcroppings, and creeks.

The most spectacular part of the Driftless Area—and the one part where the tourism does, it must be admitted, resemble or even exceed that of Door County—is the area surrounding Wisconsin Dells. The 1941 *WPA Guide to Wisconsin* captures the spirit of the Dells before it was the world's waterpark capital: "Wisconsin Dells, once called Kilbourn, changed its name in 1931 in the hope that the more descriptive title would attract tourists, for the city is a starting point for water trips up and down the Wisconsin River, here walled with carved

THE LEGEND OF THE CHEESE UNDERGROUND

Jeanne Carpenter isn't a master cheesemaker, but she may, in fact, be Wisconsin cheese's number one fan. While fandom is a highly competitive field where degrees of dedication are hard to compare apples-to-apples, consider this: in 2006 and 2007, Carpenter scheduled clandestine cheesemaker meetings for the purpose of sharing knowledge about the art.

"We'd schedule these secret meetings, at places around southwest Wisconsin," she recalls. "We would invite all the cheesemakers who were interested in affinage or building caves, for example, and we would get them all together. We'd get a bunch of cheeses that they were developing and we'd taste them."

Cheese Underground meetings would sometimes feature a speaker, and for a while the whole project was under the radar. But soon it surfaced online, albeit anonymously.

"The blog was supposed to be kind of the public piece of the cheese underground's secret meetings," Carpenter says. "But then we ended up having a meeting like only once every three months, and you can't update a blog only every three months."

Cheese Underground (cheeseunderground.com) became (and remains) one of the most vigorously updated and researched cheese blogs on the Web. It's the only blog that does the Wisconsin cheese industry—from the artisans to the megafactories—real justice. Carpenter was working for the Wisconsin Department of Agriculture when she launched the blog, but a January 2007 "outing" by the *Chicago Reader* forced her hand, and she jumped from a desk job to earning a living as a full-time writer and cheese chronicler.

Carpenter is a one-woman assault team on behalf of Wisconsin cheese. In addition to blogging for Cheese Underground, she teaches cheese classes and works with the Dairy Business Innovation Center and Wisconsin Milk Marketing Board to encourage new cheese ventures and get the word out about new developments in the industry.

Carpenter was a key player in forming the Dairy Business Innovation Center, a group that helps Wisconsinites develop specialty dairy products. While still at the Department of Agriculture, she teamed up with dairy veteran Dan Carter to get the group off the ground in 2004. "We started meeting with people, no money, no budget," she says, "and we ended up hiring Neville McNaughton."

Originally from New Zealand, McNaughton is now an American citizen and widely considered the premiere dairy technology expert in the world. "We talked him into working on a super shoestring budget, 'cause we had no money," Carpenter recalls. "We said, 'We can't pay you yet, but we're hoping we're going to get money and we'll pay you [laughs] when we get money.'"

That was good enough for McNaughton, who believed in the project's underlying vision. "He wanted to build these artisan cheese farms, help them design their building, tell them what equipment to get," she says. "We operated on almost no budget for about six or seven months. Dan Carter did not get paid for six or seven months."

The big payoff for Carpenter isn't just the cheese; it's the cheesemakers, too. "These people are so cool," she says. "I've met their families, I've eaten at their houses, I mean I've met their kids. . . . It's like this big thing in Wisconsin—once you're in, you're in. It's like you're part of an extended family."

and freakish rock. The Dells, according to Winnebago legend, were formed when a giant serpent moved southward, battering its way through great masses of rocks, leaving the land rent and broken."

Though the writer used poetic license, it's difficult to escape the feeling that some great, thoughtful force has shaped the ground in southwestern Wisconsin, protecting the land from human exploitation by folding it in on itself. It still has many of the natural features—boulders, running water, stands of trees—that are easily tamed or obliterated on the flat farmland that dominates much of the rest of the state.

Not surprisingly, the region also boasts some of the state's quirkiest masters: Sid Cook and Thomas Jenny of Carr Valley, who crank out fiercely original cheeses each year; Jake Niffenegger, the only master certified in brie, camembert, and feta; Robert Wills, whose mixed milk cheeses give everyone else's a run for their money in terms of creative firepower; Tom Torkelson, who still makes cheese from Amish canned milk; Richard Glick, a master of and tinkerer with blue and gorgonzola cheeses; and Doug Peterson, a fiercely independent cheese consultant.

Baby Cheddar, Billy Blue, and Mobay cheeses from Carr Valley Cheese Company.

Tom Torkelson

PASTURE PRIDE / NATURAL VALLEY CHEESE, Cashton, Wisconsin
http://www.pasturepridecheese.com/

Master of brick and muenster

I can never keep focused. I'm always thinking about something different. It's a curse. Seriously!

Tom Torkelson stands amid wheels of
his award-winning Cowbilly cheese.

ASK THE AVERAGE CHEESEMAKER how business is going, and most will say something fairly positive, or even downright optimistic. Tom Torkelson takes it to another level.

"We're making so many products I can't get enough vat time to get our cheeses made," he says. "I need to clone myself. I'm here three, four, five o'clock in the morning, and I'm here until five in the afternoon. I keep telling myself to take Saturday off and it just never happens."

Torkelson is the heart of one of Wisconsin's most distinctive cheese businesses. His label, Natural Valley Cheese, merged with his friend Kevin Everhart's label, Pasture Pride Cheese, in 2004. In turn, both men work with an Amish dairy cooperative called Old Country Cheese, which brings them the milk they use and owns their building. The factory, under Kevin's codirection, is K&K Cheese, named for himself and his wife, Kim.

The canned Amish milk is what gives Torkelson's cheese its flavor, its soul, and its identity. "All these farmers hand milk, and all the milk comes in the plant in cans," he says. "We have over three hundred cow milk producers and a dozen goat farmers, and our goat cheese is really starting to take off. Every day I have access to cow and goat milk."

"Access" may be understating the situation. Torkelson's plant is in the heart of an Amish settlement in Wisconsin's Kickapoo Valley. Horse-drawn buggies clippity-clop past the plant, and for miles around, all that's visible are rolling hills, green dales, little stands of trees, and healthy-looking clusters of goats and cows. Farmers' laundry flaps in the breeze, strung out on lines that stretch twenty or thirty feet.

The milk's proximity and freshness are key to the flavor of Torkelson's cheese, but it comes at a price: it requires hauling in heavy (eighty- to ninety-pound) metal cans of milk each day. The work is plenty hard, but what's harder still is finding people willing to do it each day.

But the effort, Torkelson says, is worth it. "Once I started using canned goat milk, I realized that most of the milk I was getting before was probably seven days old," he says. "Small farms comingle the milk, and it goes to this place and comes back . . . but we use our milk almost every single day to make goat cheeses, and it makes a huge difference. We have our milk delivered a lot of mornings— that's last night's milk and this morning's milk—and by afternoon we'll have that made into cheese."

Cans of Amish milk sit in a tin-smithed box. Spring water is used to cool the milk down to about fifty degrees so that it can be shipped.

Fresh milk means a fresh taste. "After that goat milk sits for three or four days, that lipase flavor comes out in that milk a little bit more, and you get that more intense goat flavor," he says. "Some of our goat cheeses—there's times when I ask: 'Is this really goat cheese?'"

Working with fresh milk from seasonal, hand-milked, grass-fed animals has its challenges, too. "I have a hard time convincing some of my artisan buyers that we make the cheese the same way, and I'm sorry that it doesn't taste exactly like it did before, you know, but it's like a wine," he says. "When spring comes, they're on pasture. Every single day, those cows have access to pasture. We actually sell some of our cheeses to co-op buyers as 'spring pasture, summer pasture, fall pasture,' and we designate certain days."

Cows pasture on different grasses, and those, in turn, supply different nutrients that make for variable flavors in the final product. "As a cheesemaker, I have to deal with real rapidly changing milk, more so than any other cheesemaker in Wisconsin," he says. "We constantly gotta make adjustments. The composition of the milk will change as the seasons change, the flavors will change. . . . As the composition changes, you have to adjust your sets and ripening time, and moistures."

Tom Torkelson is one of the few remaining cheesemakers who still works with canned milk.

Tom Torkelson's cheese is made entirely of milk from Amish farms. Many, like this one, have only eight to twelve cows.

The changing milk offers a lot of food for thought for Torkelson, who's among the state's most aggressively creative cheesemakers.

"I go to bed a lot of nights with a book in my hand," he says. "I got tons of books at home and I read about these different cultures. . . . I mean, I know them all now, but you try and find something different by adding a different culture at a different time, give it a different flavor profile. . . . In my head, I know what I could be doing with all my cheeses in two or three years."

Advice offered by artisan cheesemaker Willi Lehner took the many ideas Torkelson had brewing and multiplied them. "Willi Lehner once told me: 'I can make a vat of cheese and make five or six varieties out of that vat of cheese,'" Torkelson says. "One time he told me that and it just stuck immediately. I want to have a blooming rind aging room. . . . We've got a washed rind room. . . . I want to have a cave. . . . We need to get our own smoker."

When Torkelson looks into a vat of cheese, the possibilities are numerous—possibly even infinite. "I can take that one cheese that I make and I can put a blooming rind on it, I can put a washed rind on it, I can cave

A Tale of Three Milks

Cheese from cow's milk makes up the overwhelming majority of the cheese consumed in the United States. Typically, ten pounds of milk will yield one pound of cheese. Its relatively neutral flavor, ease of handling, and overall durability make it a (relative) pleasure to work with, although it's still subject to variability based on temperature, humidity, type of feed, and any number of other factors.

"People think 'milk in, cheese out,' but you're working with a living organism," says Gregg Palubicki of Saputo Cheese USA. "So it's got to be perfect if you want the cheese to be perfect."

Goat's milk offers a similar yield, but it is even more difficult to work with. Its shorter protein strands can make for more delicately textured cheese, but they also require far more gentle care during the cheesemaking process. Extremely fresh goat milk is a must. Older milk can create undesirable "goaty" flavor in the final product.

Sheep's milk presents its own problems. Although prodigiously rich in fat and protein (offering a yield roughly double that of cow's or goat's milk), it's expensive to produce and can be temperamental to work with.

Cow, goat, and sheep are the biggest players in the cheese world, but others have cameo roles, such as the reindeer milk–derived juustoleipa of Finland and (water) buffalo mozzarella.

Cheesemakers say that a cow's feed can have a profound impact on the milk's character and a cheese's final flavor. The milk of pasture-fed cows varies by the season, changing in fat content and imparting some of the vegetation's natural flavoring to the finished cheese.

age it, I can brine it in wine, I can brine it in beer, I can put chipotle in it, I can add fennel, I can wax it," he says. "You can make lots of kinds of cheeses out of one vat of cheese, and they're entirely different. We make four of our different cheeses out of one vat of cheese. They're just entirely different, they're not even close to the same product when they're done."

Ultimately, however, it all goes back to the milk—and the Amish farmers who produce it in a manner that would be familiar to Europeans hundreds of years ago. "If you've never been to an Amish farm and you go early in the morning when it's still dark, the kids . . . each of them has their own cow that they milk," he says. "And they sing in the morning. And I've walked in barns to drop something off or pick up a sample, and the father will be leading the kids, musically—they'll be singing! There's no machinery, so it's quiet. You'll hear the cows munching and moving around in their stanchions, and you'll hear them singing."

Tom Torkelson holds a
wheel of Cowbilly.

An Amish buggy near Cashton.

Sid Cook

Carr Valley Cheese Company, La Valle, Wisconsin
http://www.carrvalleycheese.com/

Master of cheddar and fontina

We make about sixty different cheeses. Quite a few of them are American originals.
They're cheeses that . . . well, we just make 'em up.

SID COOK, THE OWNER AND HEAD CHEESEMAKER at Carr Valley Cheese Company, is among the Wisconsin makers leading the way in new American cheeses. His personal passion for messing with mixed milks, flavors, and aging techniques has led to an explosion of new ideas in cheesemaking, and helped his company's bottom line; Carr Valley cheeses are known all over the country. But his story begins close to home.

The main Carr Valley factory is in Mauston, but the headquarters is another forty-five minutes away in La Valle, an area of small farms, quaint street names, and numerous cows. The headquarters is unassumingly small, and in December is full of cheerful employees filling mail order requests for multicolored blocks of cheese. Sid Cook gets all his milk locally, mostly within several miles of the factory. "There's a bunch of milk right around this plant, and then where my dad's plant was, there's some more farms around there. So they're clustered. . . . With the goat milk producers, we buy from eight goat milk farms. With the sheep milk we buy that through the rural Wisconsin sheep milk co-op, and that's about twelve farms."

And the cheeses Sid Cook creates are also a local enterprise. "Yes, cheesemaking has a tradition in Europe; it has a tradition in the Middle East. It has a tradition in those areas where there were cattle, sheep, goats, mares, whatever they made their dairy products, but I would really take a step away from that

TASTING NOTES: CARR VALLEY JUUSTOLEIPA

Carr Valley Cheese Company has recently started making a firm cheese based on the Finnish cheese juustoleipa that it calls bread cheese. Like a Greek halloumi or Indian paneer, it doesn't melt when heated. You can throw it on the grill or microwave it and have little squares of delicious, warm cheese.

When warm, it is salty and close to a mozzarella. The wonderful texture resembles a chunk of bread that has been soaked in cheese. The outside, which is a little browned from its production, is nutty and delicious.

European tradition where you have people coming here from Europe who are making cheeses that are really different from the ones made there.

"American cheddar is entirely different than English Cheddar. I would say that cheddar is one cheese that if you look at, say, British Cheddar it's going to be much different than Canadian, and that's going to be different than cheddar that's made in the U.S."

Sid Cook stands behind the presses for his cheese in his La Valle plant.

The flavor profiles also vary quite a bit, he says. "Say you have a cheddar that's made in Vermont or New York—you're going to have more of sulphury taste versus one that's made in California that's going to have more of caramely taste, sagey—versus one that's made in Wisconsin or Minnesota, which is going to be more fruity. It's the *terroir*," he says, referring to characteristics imparted by the local geography.

And Sid Cook's "American Original" cheeses are a testament to his belief in the unique terroir of his area. You won't find many well-known cheese names among the sixty varieties in the Carr Valley factory (although his cheddar and blue cheeses are well-known award winners)—instead, a slew of new names assault you: Benedictine, Mobay, Gran Canaria, Cocoa Cardona, Billy Blue.

Cook outlines the three ways he makes up a new cheese. "The first way is that it's just a mistake. It's a screwup, but it turns out really good. The second way is where you actually have a flavor profile that is visual, as far as your flavor memory. . . . You know what flavor you want to shoot for. And then you change all the things and use the milk or the kind of milk or culture or type of technique that you want to use to get to that goal. And the third way is to have a sort of idea of what technique you want to use, and what kind of milk you want to use, and what kind of cultures you want to use. You might not have a real clear vision of where that flavor profile is going to go, but you can tweak it at the end by how you do the affinage, what temperature, whether or not you grow bacteria on the surface, or cure it down to concentrate the flavors . . . however you do that finish on the cheese."

Cook started on his path to licensed master cheesemaker much like other cheesemakers in his

Two cows enjoy warm weather outside of Cashton.

field: he grew up in a cheese factory. "That's your life, that's how it is. My uncles and aunts all had cheese plants, my grandparents did, my great-great-uncle had a cheese plant. . . . There were many, many family personalities that owned and ran cheese plants, so whenever there was a family gathering, it was always about cheese. It was one of the topics that was talked about a great deal."

He got involved in the master cheesemaker program in the late '90s. "I had taken quite a few of the artisan courses that had been offered," he says. "There were some academics and some cheesemakers from the Netherlands, from Spain, Italy, France, Poland, Mexico, Great Britain—there was a German course—I took everything that was offered."

Sid Cook.

And although he thrived once he entered it, getting Cook committed to the program took some work up front. "Sid was a real project," recalls Bill Wendorff, a key player in the program. "He hated anything regulatory-wise. One of the problems was that Bob Bradley, my counterpart in UW Extension, pushed the ag department to require licensed pasteurizer operators. And Sid was livid. He said the university should not be in a position to put rules on industry. He wouldn't talk to us for a year or two."

Persistence paid off. "We kept working on him to get him into the master's program . . . but he was a real skeptic," Wendorff says. "After a while he started to see some of the value. Of course when he was in it, it was like a kid learning how to swim. He was great. He was one to take ideas and run with them.

"It's a challenge to try to outsmart Sid as to where he's going," Wendorff adds.

Robert Wills

CEDAR GROVE CHEESE, Plain, Wisconsin
http://www.cedargrovecheese.com/

Master of cheddar and butterkäse

The biggest challenge to good cheesemaking is letting customers know that you've done something better.

THE FIRST THING A VISITOR to the Cedar Grove Cheese plant in Plain is likely to remember is how beautiful the countryside is. Legend is that Iceland and Greenland were misleadingly named in order to confuse invaders. It's possible that Plain was named according to a similar scheme; Cedar Grove's plant is nestled in among rolling hills, streams, dales, and bucolic stretches of tree-bordered fields that recall rural Ireland more readily than the American Midwest.

The second thing a visitor to Cedar Grove is likely to recall is the plant's "Living Machine." It's a shame that a series of ten 2,600-gallon water tanks often overshadow the plant's array of excellent and unusual specialty cheeses, but there you have it: there are frogs, leeches, bluegills, plants, mosquitoes, algae, and all manner of living things running around the contained ecosystem, cleaning the plant's wastewater and impressing the pants off of the numerous visitors and apprentice cheesemakers who tramp through the plant. Although it's eco-friendly, the important thing is that it's also profitable; paying to dispose of wastewater is a constant drain on any cheesemaker's pocketbook, and the Living Machine discharges water clean enough to reuse. The cost per gallon is one-sixth what it used to be.

The man at the heart of the plant and its water-cleansing ecosystem is Robert Wills, a former state-level political operative with a law

Master cheesemaker Robert Wills of Cedar Grove Cheese shows off some of his new creations.

65

A goat from an Amish farm outside of Cashton.

Tasting Notes: Faarko

"'Faarko' comes from *far* and *ko* which are some kind of Danish words for sheep and cow," says Robert Wills. "Actually, I think it's ram and cow, but that's kind of how it goes," he adds, chuckling.

It is a smooth, softer-style cheese, rich with buttery flavor and almost fruity on the back end of the tasting, with a hint of cherry chasing its mellow, full flavor.

degree and a doctorate in economics. Despite his education credentials, Wills cites his cheesemaster's certification as one of his proudest accomplishments. "The final exam is the hardest test I ever took in my life," he says. "And that includes the PhD and law school." His secret weapon in the open book/open consultation test was Cedar Grove employee Dan Hetzel, a licensed and active cheesemaker since 1956.

There seems to be something in the air of Plain—a previous owner who sold the plant in 1946 to Wills's father-in-law still brings his friends up from Madison to visit, strolling around as if he owns the place. The visits are motivated by a love of cheesemaking that Wills is quite familiar with.

"This is probably the most exciting time in the dairy industry in Wisconsin that there's ever been," he says. "It's kind of like there's a renaissance. During history there have been these little periods when there'll be groups of writers in Paris or New York, or when Shelley and Keats and Byron and all those guys hung out together and all challenged each other, and in the music scene there's the same kind of stuff . . . and it just feels like that's what's happening in Wisconsin."

The boom in specialty cheese comes from two main factors, according to Wills. "Partly through necessity because you can't make a living here making normal cheese," he says. "And partly just because once it got rolling and there was a support system behind it, consumers got interested in what we were doing, and now people are just clamoring to see what we'll do next."

After buying the plant in 1989 (from the parents of his wife, Beth Nachreiner), the Willses transformed their business model. They diversified their customer base, went aggressively into rBGH-free and organic products, played with goat and cheese milk, and traveled to the edge of specialty experimentation.

Driven in part by a willingness to shake up old models, Wills says that the mood among Wisconsin dairymen and dairywomen has done a one-eighty.

"The first ten years I was in the business, we'd come in to work and call our friends and see who had gone out of business, and how many farms had gone down, and how many plants had closed and been bought up. . . . It was really kind of depressing," he says. "It's still challenging from a financial perspective and there are still people who go out and fail, but there's also sort of this excitement about all the new cheeses that are being made. People are pushing each other and competing, but they're doing it in such a friendly way, and they're exchanging information and collaborating on projects."

This kind of collaboration helped to bring about one of Wisconsin's most nationally celebrated cheeses, Pleasant Ridge Reserve. "[Farmer] Mike [Gingrich] came in one day, and he said, 'Look, my cows are out on pasture. I got a really select group of cows and the feed I've been giving them is really good. I've been studying cheeses around the world that are pasture-based. I want to make the best cheese in the world, and I don't care what it costs.' I said, 'Yeah, I can do that. This is my kind of project.' That 'I don't care what it costs' part was really cool."

Wills and Gingrich started working with the Center for Dairy Research in Madison, running test batches. "I think we made at least twelve different batches of about forty pounds each," says Wills. "Mike would age them in his basement and smear the surfaces, and let the rinds develop. . . . We finally came up with a cheese that we liked that was modeled roughly on a beaufort that was an Alpine fresh, high-pasture cheese during the summer months."

Cedar Grove's on-site wastewater treatment plant filters water through a system of natural materials. This "Living Machine" has become a tourist attraction unto itself.

Wills scaled it up for production at his plant. "The first year that we made it, Mike took it to the American Cheese Society down in Louisville," he says. "As he was leaving I said, 'Good luck, Mike. You're going to win the whole thing.' And he said, 'Yeah, sure.'"

Wills knows his cheese.

"He called me up two days later from Louisville, and he said, 'Bob, guess what?' I said, 'You won the whole thing.' He said, 'Yeah, I got Best in Show!' And then the cheese won Best in Show in the U.S. Championship, and then it repeated as Best in Show at the ACS, which is pretty much unheard of," says Wills. "So he started selling the stuff at twenty-eight dollars a pound and every cheesemaker on Earth and every farmer who thought he could make cheese was saying, 'Oh, I'm going to do my cheese now!'"

Wills, for his part, keeps a constantly changing rotation of cheese in his production mix.

"The core of the business is still cheese curds; we make about twenty-eight thousand pounds a week of curds," says Wills. "We start making cheese at ten o'clock at night so we can get four or five thousand pounds of curd onto trucks by seven or eight in the morning. We try to get delivery to most places twice a week so the curds are fresh. We try to make sure the ones with our label on it are the freshest out there."

Cedar Grove also puts out cheddar, grass-based during the summer months when cows are out on pasture. "Those grass-based cheeses taste better to start with," he says. "They've done blind taste tests with panels. They also have higher CLAs [conjugated linoleic acids], lower cholesterol, higher omega-3, so there are some health benefits to the grass-based cheeses—it's another one of those cooler projects where everything comes together."

Like other small makers, Wills has to stay innovative and nimble to stay viable. One of the projects in the hopper is an organic cheese "layer cake"—a layer of cheese, then a layer of flavored cheese, then another layer of cheese. Cutting into the cheese, you see bands of flavor.

"We do havarti, butterkäse, monterey jack, colby, farmer, some really nice reduced fat cheeses," he notes. "I think we were the first to put flavored curds on the market. We do horseradish, and pizza flavor, and cajun and tons of stuff. We got about a two-year head start on everybody, and then they catch up."

A certain tiny percentage of cheese curds that don't make it to market get fed to the bluegills swimming around in the Living Machine. At the end of the summer, Wills invites friends over for a curd-fattened bluegill fish fry.

Doug Peterson

DAIRYMASTERS, LLC, Mazomanie, Wisconsin
phone (608) 795-2580

Master of colby and monterey jack

I am getting pulled in many different directions right now.

THERE ARE CHEESEMAKERS WHO WOULD FEEL LOST—as though they'd had a limb lopped off—without their plants. For master cheesemaker and dairy consultant Doug Peterson, however, the experience has been tremendously liberating. As head of Dairymasters, LLC, Peterson travels the country—and world—tackling dairy problems with his unique brand of experience and plainspoken bluntness.

"I used to work for a large dairy cooperative, and I was a plant manager," he says. "I hated dealing with employees and day-to-day boring stuff. I transferred into their research and development. I did that for six years for them. They are a good company, but I saw how they run million-pound, two-million-pound plants. They make one product all day long. I was thinking, 'Man, that is not me,' so I moved on."

He grins. "Now I get to mess in just about every kind of thing there is.

"My smallest client runs a five-thousand-pound vat, one a day; my largest client runs two million pounds a day," he says. "I've got that high-automated high-volume experience, and I've got that hands-on, make-it-in-the-bathroom experience. So it is good for me." He points to his head. "A lot of things going on up here—that's why I like it so much."

Doug Peterson.

Peterson developed a cheese that can stand up to high-temperature pizza ovens, and he oversees its production at the Mullins cheese plant in the central part of the state. He's also the operations consultant for the Wisconsin Farmers Union Specialty Cheese Company Montfort plant, a blue cheese operation, and two other colby–monterey jack operations.

Peterson and his family had a direct hand in the creation of cojack, the colorful marbled blend of yellow colby and white monterey jack that is one of the most popular cheeses on the market today. Peterson, his father, and his brother-in-law all were involved in the magic moment.

A scenic view along highways 162 and 33.

"We were making colby and monterey jack," he recalls. "Basically during cleanup, my brother-in-law was always screwing around rather than working. So he mixes them together and presses them together and yells, 'That's cojack!' My dad picked some up and sold it in our retail store and it sold really fast. We made a lot of it. We had a trademark on the name and a patent on the process, because we made it in one vessel. We went a long time with that, and then Kraft got it in and called it colby-jack. We didn't have a million dollars to sue Kraft, so we kind of lost it."

While business is booming for Peterson, who seems to be trying to juggle several dozen projects at once, he worries about the state of the Wisconsin dairy industry. "My opinion is that the industry in Wisconsin has been really beaten up and banged around," he says. "The value of whey found itself on the milk price, and put a lot of these small- to medium-sized plants at a disadvantage. It has been really tough the last five years watching that. A lot of the plants that had the capability of putting in whey processing saw some of this coming apparently, and they are doing well."

Peterson points at two high-profile buyouts in early 2008 as an example of where the cheese business has suffered. "Agropur came in and bought Trega Foods, Saputo came in and bought Alto, which was a milk cooperative," he says. "When you think about a private company coming in and buying a milk cooperative, that is disastrous in my opinion for dairy farmers in Wisconsin. That is thousands of producers now not being represented by their own interests."

Over time, he says, there have been some important steps forward for the industry, but they've come at a price. "There have been huge improvements of consistency," he concedes. But, he adds, "I think the industry has lost some very good traditional cheeses. For example, colby used to be real tender and have a lot of openings in it. The automated boys lobbied the regulators, and now it is a cheese that lost its identity. Very few consumers really care about it anymore."

Jake Niffenegger

Lactalis USA, Belmont, Wisconsin
http://www.presidentcheese.com/

Master of brie, camembert, and feta

We used to cut all the vats by hand with wire knives, and now we have a robot that cuts them.
It's pretty neat. When it's working.

JAKE NIFFENEGGER SEEMS LIKE AN OLD HAND at making brie and camembert, and indeed he is—he's been working for Lactalis USA in Belmont since 1984. But when he first arrived at the European-style factory, he was in for some culture shock.

"It was pretty wild," he recalls. "I was pretty young when I started at Lactalis, and I'd been making cheddar and colby. I was used to making cheese in thirty-thousand-pound vats. I'd bucket and shovel the curd."

Things were different at the new plant.

"I walked in the making room," he recalls, "and they had probably about a hundred little white tubs sitting on the floor, and I'm going, 'Where are your big vats?' And they said, 'These are our vats right here.' And I'm going, 'OK . . .'"

The tiny vats hold only about three hundred pounds of milk. "That's to control the quantity of curd that goes into each mold as you're molding it," he says. "Then after you make the cheese, you're wondering how you press the cheese, and they go, 'No, we don't do that here.' It's all the draining rooms and the force of gravity; the whey comes out of the curd and it just kind of fuses itself together because the curd's a lot softer than cheddar and colby."

Things weren't any less strange in the curing rooms, where hundreds of puffy white wheels of cheese line the shelves. Each cheese has what appears to be a white fur coat of cottonlike mold on it, fluffing out from the rind like the puff on a dandelion and wrapping itself around the metal bars of the racks. The mold is eventually packed down to make brie's familiar white exterior, but while it ages, it looks a bit alien. And it takes time. "To make one day's cheese, it takes eight or nine days," he says.

Niffenegger is, by necessity, a different breed of cheesemaker from some of his big-company colleagues who talk about pounding out tons and slamming cheese through the line. Brie is delicate stuff, particularly when it's still in its feather-light curd stage.

"You've got to do a lot of babysitting with it," he says. "Close monitoring of it all the time. You've got to make sure your curing rooms maintain a certain temperature and a certain humidity for the aging of the cheese to make the mold grow. Sometimes it'll be a little softer and you need to take another day to just dry it out a little bit."

Jake Niffenegger displays four bries at different stages of mold formation.

If you've had brie, you've probably had Niffenegger's, which—like the camembert made for Lactalis under the Président brand name—is mildly flavored to suit the American palate. Americans don't (yet, anyway) tend to like stinky cheese, and Président isn't stinky. It's also a beautiful cheese.

"It has a nice, smooth texture," says Niffenegger. "You can cut the piece of cheese, you can hold it off to the side and let the light shine off of the product and it'll have a nice, shiny texture to it—smooth, creamy. You'll have a few little mechanical holes you can see in the product, which is good."

Jake Niffenegger displays samples of
brie made at Lactalis USA.

Left at room temperature, the cheese practically begs to be spread on a slice of warm bread. "If you cut the piece of cheese and set it on a plate at room temperature for an hour or so, you can see it sort of sag out a little bit," he says. "Not ooze out, like Velveeta or something. Just sag a bit."

The delicate nature of the cheese—it lasts only six or eight weeks on a shelf, as opposed to cheddars, which can happily wander up into the double digits when properly made and aged—led Lactalis to set up shop in Belmont. Ship cheese across the Atlantic, and it loses weeks of life. Make it here, and you can distribute it far more economically.

The result is a Wisconsin cheese plant that, perhaps more than any other, resembles Willy Wonka's chocolate factory. White plastic pyramidal vats trundle along a line powered by white plastic tracks pulled by gleaming stainless steel chains; a massive robot arm covered with some manner of fabric cuts curd with a screen, looking like an oversized sock puppet in the process; workers flip aging cheese by hand, up to four or five times per cheese before it ships.

Niffenegger suspects that he'll be the only one in his family to preside over the slightly surreal brie, camembert, and feta paradise that is the Belmont plant. "I have three daughters and they're not going to make cheese," he says. "My middle daughter worked in a lab one summer. . . . 'How the heck can you stand working there? It stinks!'"

Thomas Jenny

CARR VALLEY CHEESE COMPANY, Mauston, Wisconsin
http://www.carrvalleycheese.com/

Master of swiss

You do conventional cheesemaking for a while, and after a while you kind of want to change things.

THOMAS JENNY WAS LIVING A LIFE THAT, for a Wisconsin cheesemaker, was fairly typical. He was making swiss cheese, learning about the industry from his father and uncle, living near Platteville (he worked in the area for thirty-three years), and doing his best to survive the periodic buyouts and plant closings that dogged the industry.

Then he got a call from a friend who'd worked at his dad's cheese plant in Platteville—master cheesemaker Sid Cook. "He called me up one day at the last place I worked," says Jenny, "and asked me how I was doing. I said, 'Eh, I'm not really happy with what I'm doing here,' and he said, 'Come work with me.' He'd been after me for ten years."

Jenny made the jump in 2004, coming over to run Cook's Mauston cheese plant. According to Jenny, Cook's style has changed the way he looks at cheesemaking. "Sid does a lot of unique things with cheese that had never even dawned on me," says Jenny. "Talking to him and through the grapevine I'd heard he was making some new stuff with goat and sheep's milk. I'd never worked with sheep before I came here—my specialty was cow. Like everybody's," he adds. "It was kind of a learning curve for me, and that was kind of exciting for me. I needed a change. And he's a fun guy to work with."

Part of the fun—and the intimidation factor—of working with Cook is his willingness to roll the dice on cheesemaking. "Right after

Thomas Jenny, with a wheel of
Carr Valley cheese.

75

I'd started working for Sid, he said, 'Make me a vat of swiss.' I knew that was going to happen. He'd been buying swiss, and I know he didn't want to buy it if he could make it. It'd been three or four years since I'd last made it, so I said, 'Let me think about it.'

"A couple months later, he said, 'Decided what to do?' I said sure, and he said, 'How much milk are you planning to use?' I said, 'Maybe about five thousand pounds.' 'Oh, use a whole vat,' he said. 'You want me to use seventeen thousand pounds of milk? What if it doesn't turn out?' 'We'll just call it something and sell it in the store.'"

Carr Valley Cheese Company is known for its "American Original" cheeses.

Another one of the unusual challenges of being part of the Carr Valley Cheese Company team is dealing with sheep's milk. "Sheep milk has a lot more fat in it," Jenny says. "Sheep yield is probably a sixteen-[pound] yield [per hundred pounds of milk]; regular cow milk is like ten. It's almost a hundred dollars a hundred [pounds], too—you don't want to spill it," he says with a laugh.

"You can get five thousand pounds in and it costs you an arm and a leg, but you can charge more for it—it gives you more yield and it gives you a different taste," he adds. "And a lot of people don't mess with sheep cheese. Sid is kind of on the forefront of that. He was making cheddar all them years and he knew he wasn't going to be able to survive on it."

Right after sheep's milk, the toughest thing Jenny has to wrangle on a regular basis is his staff. "The work ethic has changed," he says. "The generation nowadays think they deserve this, and they don't have to work for it. The stuff kids get away with nowadays, twenty years ago you couldn't. It's hard to keep help, too. Not everybody wants to make cheese."

Jenny has a unique bragging right when it comes to the master cheesemaker program: "I was actually the first to get my ring and my medal," he says. "So I was the first one and only one for about fifteen seconds."

Jenny says he takes pride in Wisconsin's unique status as a state with a master cheesemaker program—it reflects a mentality that helps set the state aside from commodity producers. "Bruce Workman and Jeff Wideman and I were having a beer one night after one of the conventions, and this guy from California came in," he recalls. "And we're always ribbin' each other, you know. And he had—he was feelin' pretty good. 'What makes you guys think you're better cheesemakers than us?' Jeff goes, 'Well, you see the three of us? That's ninety-five years of cheesemaking experience. Can you say that?' Well, no. 'And if we aren't any good, why are you coming to Wisconsin and making all our cheesemakers move out there?' He didn't have much to say about that. He just got up and walked away."

A cow near Ontario, Wisconsin.

Richard Glick

Swiss Valley Farms (retired), still consulting, La Farge, Wisconsin
http://www.swissvalley.com/

Master of blue and gorgonzola

Nowadays, a cheesemaker lets computers do it for him. But a true cheesemaker uses his hands to do it.

"I was born and raised on a dairy farm," says master cheesemaker Richard Glick. "This is the farm." He gestures off toward the green hill that rises dramatically above La Farge, a town of fewer than a thousand people not far from La Crosse. Family is one of the keys to cheesemaking, from Glick's perspective—his uncle, Gerald Glick, owned and operated a small plant called Warner Creek Cheese not far from La Farge. "He took me under his wing and taught me a lot about cheese," Glick recalls. "Making the best cheese was always his goal. He took pride in the product he made and taught me to do the same."

Glick built his career making a variety of Wisconsin classics, such as cheddar and muenster, but he came into his own with a couple special varieties of blue and gorgonzola cheese. But before he arrived at the peak of his career as a master cheesemaker at Swiss Valley Farms, where he would make a blue cheese that would win praise on national television, he logged some hard hours in old-fashioned Wisconsin cheese plants.

"It was all canned milk at that time, so you know how long I've been around," he says, grinning. "The cheese-making job then—and I don't think people would work this way today—you went to work and you didn't go home until it was done. Usually going to work was three in the morning, and it was a twelve-hour day."

The work was more physical, too. "Some of us cheesemakers would haul milk, because you couldn't store it overnight—you couldn't get it refrigerated down enough," he says. "So the milk had to come in, and then you had to make the cheese before you went home."

After getting his license under the tutelage of cheese guru Mike Dean in 1966, Glick went through a variety of jobs, including one at a plant in Hillsboro. "We made muenster there, and mild brick," he says. "We developed that plant into the largest muenster plant in the country at that time. Eighteen percent of the country's muenster came out of that Hillsboro plant then."

In 1997 he started working with Swiss Valley at its Mindoro plant. Volume was initially slender—two vats of blue cheese a day—but Glick would help adapt the traditionally Continental cheese into a domestic powerhouse.

"We monkeyed around with our blue cheese," he says. "That's one thing a master cheesemaker has to ask: What if? What if we'd changed this or done that—what would happen? And I think that's a profile of master cheesemakers, in two words: what if?"

A blend of two cultures mixed into the milk (rather than injected)—along with rich, full whole milk flavor—made all the difference for the Mindoro cheese's unique profile. "It had a pronounced flavor that grabbed you right at the front, but then it mellowed off and had a creamy flavor," Glick says. "That was with the whole milk; it was real creamy. We made a lot of blue cheese for other companies—and they still do. When I was going through the master's program, I remember the grader saying, 'Richard, you won't win a lot of medals with this blue cheese, but it's the best blue cheese I've ever tasted.' Because ours was different, a nontraditional blue."

What Glick did with blue, he repeated with another relatively exotic cheese. "Then we worked with the Center for Dairy Research, because we were going to make gorgonzola," he says. "We looked at the true gorgonzola recipe, and we

Richard Glick displays his collection of antique processed-cheese boxes.

didn't want to do that exactly. So we dropped the moisture, and did a little different process on the front of that gorgonzola and developed our own type. We called it 'U.S. Gorg.' That got off the ground real quick."

The job took a great deal of energy, and Glick credits his wife, Gloria, for not merely tolerating his career choice, but actively encouraging him and understanding the long hours demanded of those who make great cheese.

Although Glick is semiretired after more than forty-three years of making cheese, his reputation has attracted attention from folks who would like to pull him back into the game. "I have California beating on my door pretty hard right now," he says. "Martha Stewart liked our [blue cheese], and said it was the best. She said, 'There's some little cheese plant out in the country called Mindoro that makes the best blue cheese, and we'll use it in this recipe.'"

It's that process of constant tinkering and analysis—guided by deep experience and well-honed intuition—that for Glick defines a true master of the art.

"I mean, everybody could make cheddar with a machine," he scoffs. "But the guys who develop their own product—Sid Cook's a good friend of mine, and Tom [Torkelson] is a good friend of mine, and they're always thinking: 'what if?' That's what I'm always saying: 'what if?'

"Nowadays, a cheesemaker lets computers do it for him," Glick says. "But a true cheesemaker uses his hands to do it. At the time I got my master's, I told them it was the best program there could be in the United States. I've had people comment, you know . . . you've got Super Bowl winners with Super Bowl rings, and nobody really

thinks about these guys who put their heart to something special."

Obtaining his master's certification for blue and gorgonzola cheeses was more than a professional achievement for Glick. "What convinced me to be a master cheesemaker is that I wanted one thing at the end of my life, when I retired, so that I could say, 'Hey, I was one of the best.' That's really what was my goal. And so I went for it."

Richard Glick, wearing his master cheesemaker's ring.

Gary Grossen

Babcock Hall Dairy Plant, Madison, Wisconsin
http://foodsci.wisc.edu/services/dairy/

Master of brick and muenster

When it's the end of the day and the plant is just shiny and clean, you think,
"Now I know why I got up so early this morning."

Gary Grossen and his award-winning gouda.
The cheese is aged in the cellar of Babcock
Hall at the University of Wisconsin.

ANYONE WHO DOUBTS THE SINCERITY of the University of Wisconsin's connection to the farmers and dairymen of the state should stop by and visit with Gary Grossen. As the cheesemaker at Babcock Hall Dairy Plant, part of the university's Department of Food Science, he supervises the production of the dairy products sold on campus and a few local stores, and serves as a mentor to young cheesemakers seeking their state licenses. And while his work interfaces with research and educational aspects of the department's overall mission, he did the requisite career building out in the field, at his family's Green County cheese plant, Prairie Hill.

"For fifty-one years I lived above that cheese factory, until 2001," he says. "I'm the real McCoy cheesemaker. We were born and raised into it. Through all the years, my mother and father raised us kids there. You just lived right up above the factory and you knew when everything was running right. The boiler was running and the pipes were clanging . . . and at a very young age you had duties to do."

Like many of Wisconsin's master cheesemakers, he credits a childhood structured around man-sized chores as the bedrock of his work ethic and understanding of how to work with milk.

"Back when I started out, we still had canned milk," he says. "It wasn't bulk trucks—it was cans. One of my first jobs was painting the number on the outside. Each farmer had his own number."

When Grossen was a kid, Monroe, Wisconsin, was still to a large extent the center of the American cheese universe. Buyers and distributors crowded the town. "On Tuesdays is when we would take the cheese into Monroe," he recalls. "You had all these buyers—you had Armor and Company and Monroe Cheese Corporation and Swiss Colony and on and on and on, and Tuesday was the day we all got in the cheese truck and there was

A sign in Babcock Hall Dairy Plant celebrates Gary Grossen's gouda and election as king of Green County's Cheese Days festival.

five of us in that one seat. And you just went to town that day and you did everything. You hauled cheese and went grocery shopping and maybe us kids would get to go swimming, and then back home we'd go. After unloading cheese, Pop would have to go and have a couple refreshments, you know," he says, eyes twinkling.

Despite the relatively relaxed pace of his work at Babcock, Grossen isn't slacking from a cheese quality perspective, particularly where gouda is concerned. If you visit the university's plant and look down at the tanks, vats, and hoses from the observation deck, you'll see a relatively small place, buzzing with activity. In one corner of the floor, there's a chalkboard that bears a message written by a student half in jest, half sincerely: "Gary Grossen: Gouda King."

"This year, I got to boast a little bit. I placed third in the world with the gouda," he says. "And last year I placed first in the U.S. with it. What I want to do here. . . . See, back at Prairie Hill we had world and U.S. awards and state fair awards on our muenster and brick. That's what I'm certified in [as a master cheesemaker]. I'm going through for cheddar. Then after that I'd like to do the gouda, and probably another one."

When Grossen takes visitors on a tour of his gouda aging room, he beams with pride at the brilliant yellow poly-coated wheels that line the shelves. "This gouda thing, it's been fantastic. Walt Brandli, he did a very very very good job on the gouda here," he says, referring to the master cheesemaker who preceded him at Babcock. "He started making it here."

Between teaching up-and-coming cheesemakers and working the CDR, Grossen says he doesn't lack for duties, despite the plant's relative lack of size. "I make every day, but I got things to do in between," he says. "With gouda, I've got poly-coating to do. I keep awful busy here. My vat down here is 5,000 pounds. I'm doing 5,000 pounds a day when I used to do 120,000 pounds. But I'm keeping so busy."

Grossen's Green County track record makes him a perfect fit for a university setting, where education and collaboration tend to come ahead of sheer productivity.

"The people I had working for me—you'd never hear me call them hired men, because they weren't," he says. "I had five of my main people that were there with me twenty or thirty years, and they all had come up in cheesemaking. There's one thing, people ask me: 'How'd you keep these guys for so long?' We were all Indians, and no chiefs. Was I the owner and manager and whatever you want to call me? Yeah. But them guys were experienced, too. We'd get together and I'd ask, 'What do you think?' I'm proud to say that now them people have gone on and they're still in the cheesemaking business."

Grossen's track record hasn't gone unnoticed. In 2008 he and his wife, Corie, were named king and queen of Green County Cheese Days. "Out of all the people that are worthy of this title, it's very very rewarding that they asked us," he says.

Was your wife pretty excited?

"Oh my God, she bawled."

The landscape outside of Plain.

The Masters
OF SOUTHEASTERN WISCONSIN

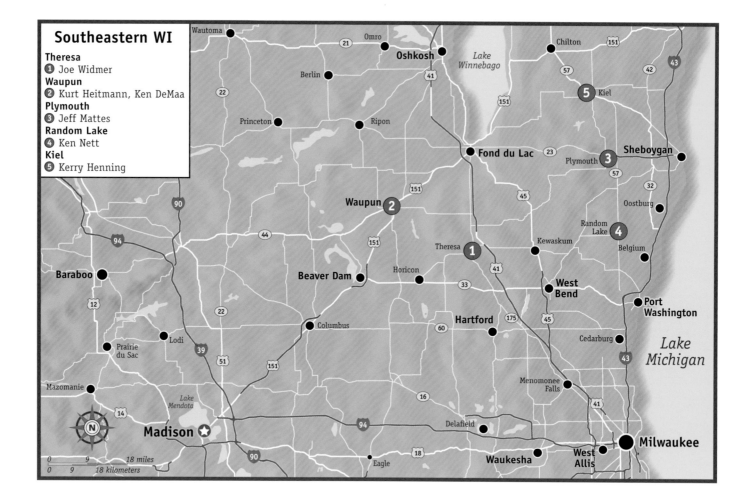

Southeastern WI

Theresa
① Joe Widmer
Waupun
② Kurt Heitmann, Ken DeMaa
Plymouth
③ Jeff Mattes
Random Lake
④ Ken Nett
Kiel
⑤ Kerry Henning

Wautoma
Omro
Oshkosh
Berlin
Lake Winnebago
Chilton
Kiel ⑤
Princeton
Ripon
Fond du Lac
Plymouth ③ Sheboygan
Oostburg
Waupun ②
Random Lake ④
Belgium
Theresa ①
Kewaskum
Beaver Dam
Horicon
West Bend
Baraboo
Port Washington
Columbus
Hartford
Cedarburg
Lake Michigan
Prairie du Sac
Lodi
Mazomanie
Menomonee Falls
Lake Mendota
Delafield
Madison
Eagle
Waukesha
West Allis
Milwaukee

0   9   18 miles
0   9   18 kilometers

IF YOU GO TO SOUTHEASTERN WISCONSIN, you're probably primed to eat, drink, and be merry. Milwaukee's brewing heritage lives on through midsized artisan brewers, such as Sprecher and Lakefront; Sheboygan is still the spiritual home of the bratwurst; and when in Racine you must—absolutely must—pick up some of the city's famous Danish kringle. So it follows that cheesemaking would have deep roots in this part of the state.

As one of the most densely populated and developed parts of Wisconsin, with generations upon generations of commerce and settlement, it's no surprise that master cheesemakers here are among the most deeply traditional and family focused of any in the state. At Widmer's Cheese Cellars, tradition is conveyed by every make procedure, and by the antique bricks that are stacked on top of the brick cheese; Henning's Wisconsin Cheese is a family operation through and through, a partnership that turns out uniquely massive "mammoth" cheddar cheeses, among others; and master cheesemaker Ken Nett works side by side with his son at Cedar Valley Cheese, where he makes, among other things, some of the best string cheese in the state.

PROCESS CHEESE

Process (or "processed") cheese runs the gamut from cheese spreads, which combine little more than milk, cream, and high quality cheese, to "cheese foods" or "cheese products," which are a mixture of low-grade cheese and large proportions of whey, emulsifiers, milk, flavorings, colorings, and other additives. Spreads such as Rondelé or Alouette are closer to the former, and Cheez Whiz and Velveeta are on the other end of the spectrum.

The act of making processed cheese kills off (and thereby halts the activity of) the bacteria at work. Consequently, processed cheese won't age and change in your fridge but it will eventually go bad.

The art of making a good process cheese, such as the ones sold in earthenware crocks at traditional cheese plants, presents its own challenges and secrets, such that the CDR's Jim Path had hoped to develop formal recognition for its masters. It was not to be. "I was kind of hoping we could have a mastership in process cheese," Path says. "I could not get those old cheesemakers on board. . . . That was a brick wall."

Kurt Heitmann and Ken DeMaa at Waupun's enormous Saputo Cheese USA plant (formerly Alto Dairy Cooperative) approach cheesemaking from a larger scale, a perspective that also has historical roots in southeastern Wisconsin.

In the late 1920s Kraft purchased the Pabst brewing corporation, acquiring a product called Pabst-ett in the process. This cheese and whey spread, developed as a partial solution to the whey disposal problem, would eventually become Velveeta (the scientist who developed it figured out its method for concentrating whey protein at the Pabst brewery in Milwaukee). As the decades rolled by, processed cheese and concentrated whey proteins would both become massively important to the bottom line of the state's dairy industry.

Joe Widmer

WIDMER'S CHEESE CELLARS, Theresa, Wisconsin
http://www.widmerscheese.com/

Master of brick and colby

You saw my guys out at the vats flipping the cheese—a lot of that's done with machines now at other plants.
We're still leaning over the vats. What do you want, Grandma's doughnuts, or Dunkin' Donuts?

WITH THE ADDITION OF THE RIGHT MUSIC—something with a manic
tempo—the action that takes place in Widmer's Cheese Cellars would
resemble an elaborately choreographed dance number. Workers make a
series of repeated motions: cheesemaker Joe Widmer's tossing of metal
plates onto brick cheese forms like a Vegas veteran dealing cards; the
"stack, drain, cut, stack, cut, stack, mill" routine of old-fashioned
cheddaring; and at the end of the number, the soaping and rinsing
of the vats.

The physical motion that defines the plant is constant, but
economical—you get the feeling that the guys doing it have everything
calculated, on a gut level, down to the last angle. Widmer says that much
of the plant's strength comes from its traditional methods, and good
old-fashioned elbow grease. "As far as make process, we've stayed pretty
much the same," says Widmer, the third generation of his family to
run the plant. "We're pretty adamant about sticking to tradition for two
reasons: we get a lot of tourism here, and we believe it makes a better
product."

The plant's traditional look and feel are built at least in part on the
old bricks. When not in use, they sit in neat piles on shelves hung from
wall-mounted chains. "My grandpa [John Widmer] bought a set of bricks

Joe Widmer presses his brick cheese
with actual bricks.

when he started making brick cheese," says Widmer. "We're still using the bricks my grandfather bought in 1922. We're making cheese like the Flintstones." When they crack from use, "we glue 'em," he says. "He came over in 1905. It sounds like an easy thing, but you're leaving your whole family behind: mom, dad, brothers, sisters. So he had a job lined up about ten miles from here working as an apprentice in a cheese factory. That's where he learned to make cheese. That was 1905."

Although John Widmer left Switzerland behind in order to make cheese in America, he kept in touch with a girlfriend by mail. In 1911 she announced her plans to come over to join him in the United States and asked if he

Bricks press additional whey out of brick cheese, helping it age more gracefully.

could meet her in New York. This wasn't a trivial journey at the time, but John Widmer agreed, and headed out to the port of New York.

"This ship came in, and about half the people got off," Joe Widmer says. "And she was still up there, and so he says to these guys, 'What's going on?' They said, 'We've filled our quota, these people have no visa, and they have no business here, so we're sending them back.' He said, 'My girlfriend's up there. How can I get her off the ship?'"

"By marrying her," he was told. "In Wisconsin?" he asked. "Right on the dock," came the reply. And so he did. "They honeymooned in New York for a week, and they came back to Wisconsin," says Widmer.

And although two generations have gone by, Joe Widmer maintains a cheesemaking tradition that is profoundly aligned with its original European heritage. You can taste the difference, he insists. "You could process at a higher temperature to make brick, but that changes the moisture," Widmer says. "Instead, we cool it like an old-fashioned brick was and then press it with bricks. A lot of time with cheddar manufacturing, back in the olden days, we'd wash the curd to remove excess whey and we still do that. You have to remove the excess whey because it has lactose in it, and the bacteria converts lactose into lactic acid. If you're making an aged cheddar, the more sugar you have, the older it gets, the more it converts the sugar, and it gets bitter."

Brick cheese curds are scooped into forms by hand.

The brick and colby cheeses made by Widmer are revelations. Made by many other plants, both varieties have become bland, debased versions of the old Wisconsin original cheeses for which they are named. (Brick cheese was developed by John Jossi in the 1870s; Colby was developed by Joseph F. Steinwand, near Colby, in 1885.)

But sample either at Widmer's Cheese Cellars, and you'll be moved by the difference. Widmer's brick is a full-flavored washed rind cheese with all the complexity and depth of a European soft cheese. Paired with strong

All the cheddar made at Widmer's Cheese Cellars is hand cheddared, a labor-intensive process in which the curds are allowed to knit together and are stacked before they are milled and pressed into forms.

mustard and sweet onions, it holds its flavor and becomes the lead note in a powerful trio of flavor. It's known by some as "the married man's limburger"—pungent, but nonlethal.

"My uncle Ralph always told a story about the farmers around here—when he made brick he'd always put a piece aside for them, and hold onto it until it just about walked," says Widmer. "So then these guys go out and they marry a girl from the city, and they come home from the honeymoon. He goes out and buys that brick, puts it in the refrigerator, and she comes home and throws it out. They get in their first fight over cheese," he says with a laugh.

Colby, for its part, has become confused in the public mind with a mild—bland, frankly—cheddar. But traditional colby is quite a different animal. "The acid's not allowed to go as high as the cheddar," says Widmer. "Now, with cheddar, I often let it go up to a sixty or seventy titratable acidity; that's how long I let the bacteria work. With the colby, we stop it at like twenty, and it's in a granular form. It's a completely different cheese."

How to Cheddar the Cheese

Cheddar cheese is traditionally made through a tiring process known as cheddaring. In order to control moisture in the curd, the curd is cut and whey is drained off. Water is added to the curd and heated under constant stirring. The curds are heated to around one hundred degrees so they begin to melt together, and then the water is drained off. At this point, the curd is pushed with rakelike tools into long banks lining the side of the vat to release the excess whey. The curds knit together until they form heavy sheets that are cut into loaves with machetelike knives to release more whey. The loaves are stacked atop one another in order to compress the curd further and squeeze out yet more moisture. Next, they are flipped and stacked multiple times over the course of several hours until they flatten out into almost pancakelike mats of cheese. At this point, the mats are cut into slices and the heavy pieces are fed through a mill, thus creating the "cheese curds" Wisconsinites know and love. They can be eaten as is or pressed into forms to create cheddar suitable for aging.

Cheddar can also be made through a stirred-curd process using a mechanical agitator. Machine-made cheddar can be plenty good, but it doesn't necessarily age out as well. The excess whey (which contains lactose) can lead to a sharper ammonia flavor as it ages.

In the '80s, colby suffered a sad transformation at the hands of the government. While the United States Department of Agriculture (USDA) has done much to protect the cheese industry by insisting on high standards of safety and sanitation, it also bears the responsibility for cheapening the identity of a Wisconsin original cheese.

"When the mechanization of cheddar came out in the '80s, a lot of the same guys who made colby made cheddar, and they found out there was a little similarity between a mild cheddar and colby," says Widmer.

"So they started making mild cheddar and calling it colby. They're two different cheeses, but the USDA sided with them [the makers], and changed the definition of colby."

Widmer's pain over the decision is still palpable. "They hurt an American original by doing that, because it's not an original cheese anymore," he says. "We still make an original one, and there's a couple other factories in Wisconsin that make an original colby."

True colby is softer and moister than cheddar; the spraying of cold water on the curds while they're still in the vat stops them from knitting together completely, and gives the cheese a more elastic, open texture that is perforated with tiny holes.

It's an open question who will safeguard these unique cheeses down the line. Widmer is a vigorous guy, but he can't work the vats forever. He worries about the future, and particularly the work ethic among the younger generation. "It's harder to find people," he says. "Less and less kids have had to do manual labor and intensive work. We've got a young guy in now who's doing very well, but it was very tough for him at first, because he never had to do a lot of hands-on work, all that bending and lifting."

That said, there could be future Widmers in the business. "My son's eighteen, and he's not real sure what he wants to do," says Joe. "I told him, more or less, follow your heart. Don't do it because you think you have to carry on the business. Don't do it because you think there's money in it. Do it because you love it, or don't do it. And I have a twelve-year-old daughter who spends time down here and likes it, so I'm not sure."

A pond in Steinhall, Wisconsin.

Kurt Heitmann and Ken DeMaa

Saputo Cheese USA (formerly Alto Dairy Cooperative), Waupun, Wisconsin
http://www.saputousafoodservice.com/alto_site4.html

Masters of cheddar and mozzarella (Heitmann and DeMaa), colby and monterey jack (Heitmann)

It just fascinated me, watching how the vats would set and coagulate. It was kind of neat, you know!
—KURT HEITMANN

LIKE MANY—OR, REALLY, MOST—of those who have risen to the top of the Wisconsin cheese industry, Kurt Heitmann worked his way up with a soapy rag and ample amounts of elbow grease. He got his cheesemaker's license in 1976.

"When I first came [to Alto—now owned by Saputo Cheese USA Inc.], I started in the plant doing cleanup. Cleanup was always at night, so I was always in scrubbing, making sure things were clean, taking equipment apart. My job actually was CIP [clean-in-place], so I used to wash the outside of equipment, taking care of milk separators, tearing them apart to make sure they were all clean."

Curiosity took hold, and Heitmann stuck with the job. He worked his way through the plant, jumping from job to job, eventually learning how to make the bacterial starter that is key to determining the final characteristics of most cheeses.

Heitmann uses his now encyclopedic knowledge of cheesemaking to help run what is currently the biggest cheese plant east of the Mississippi. The Waupun plant goes through about 4.0 million pounds of milk a day, split up between the two subplants; the smaller plant runs about 1.6 million, and the larger handles the rest.

Ken DeMaa, at the Saputo Cheese USA (formerly Alto) plant in Waupun.

Even in the seventies, the Alto Waupun plant was running a million pounds of milk, meaning that consistency was key. And key to consistency is understanding the life cycles, habits, pet peeves, and mischievous whims of the bacterial starter culture that gives cheese its characteristic flavors and physical characteristics.

"When I started making the starter, I began to learn about bacteria," he recalls. "That part still fascinates me to this day. Every bacteria is different, has its own characteristics, and I treat each one differently. If I put one in milk and five or ten minutes earlier than normal it starts eating the lactose, I'll map that all out for the guys. Sometimes we all have a bad day. Sometimes it wasn't the bacteria's problem."

The inside of a large vat of milk at Saputo's Waupun plant.

When Heitmann talks about his starter a note of real affection creeps into his voice. "Every bacteria has its own personality," he says. "They're living organisms. I always tell guys in the plant when I give them cheesemaking classes: 'It's like a pet dog.'"

Part of the responsibility for owning a pet is keeping it healthy. As strange as it may sound, a bacteria can get "sick" when it is overwhelmed by a kind of virus known as bacteriophage—the name is derived from *bacteria* and the Greek *phagein* (to eat).

"Phage is a virus that attacks the bacteria—with phage, it'll get ahold of a bacteria and inject its DNA into it, so when that bacteria splits instead of making more bacteria it makes phage," Heitmann says. "Instead of one bacteria splitting and making two bacteria, when it splits it might make thirty or a hundred more phage. If you don't have a lot of bacteria there, it's going to kill everything and you'll have a dead vat—you won't have any bacteria alive."

If Heitmann charts the course for the plant, fellow master cheesemaker Ken DeMaa drives the car.

"[Kurt's] considered the brains behind it," DeMaa says. "And we have a very good working relationship. He's on that end of it, and I'm on the floor end of things, executing it. I try to work every day with my people: 'This is why we

Kurt Heitmann grading cheddar.

do what we do.' To them it's just a routine thing, but there's a reason behind every step that we take, and I try to pass that on to the people that are on the floor."

As a floor supervisor, DeMaa is focused on the end product: the cheese turned out and shipped off by the semi-load. But although the Waupun plant produces on a mind-blowing scale, the quality is what caught DeMaa's eye. "The big one for me was the product that we produced," he says. "Back then, the United States government was using our cheese in world cheese competitions. And that's what sparked it off. I knew what we made was the best the United States had to offer. And I wondered: Why would it happen here at Alto?"

Kurt Heitmann manages many of the operations at the largest cheese plant east of the Mississippi.

Sanitation and the culture program were important, he discovered. But, not surprisingly, the source ingredient was a major player in making quality cheese. "Of course it begins with the milk, and the criteria that they put on the farmers to produce high-quality milk," he says. "And then it all kind of fit, and I became more interested, and I thought, 'Jeez, I want to run the vats! I want to be the cheesemaker!'"

After DeMaa has worked with the line to make the cheese, the process is juggled back over to Heitmann, who works with a veteran crew of licensed graders to assess the product. "I'm a licensed grader myself, and I have two guys who are licensed graders who work for me—one of them has been here for thirty-some years and the other forty, so they know each other's minds," Heitmann says. "I'll take that information and match it up to the bacteria that was being used and then set up the schedule for how I'm going to use it the next time in the plant, and how am I going to run it."

In addition to the old-school help available in house, Heitmann draws on the team behind the master cheesemaker program when a particular problem gets tough. "If I need to, I can go to the phone and call up Mark Johnson at the Center for Dairy Research or John Jaeggi," Heitmann says. "Dean Sommer works for the Center for Dairy Research and he used to be my boss. I still talk to Dean and we bounce things off each other. I can call these guys up any time, day or night—they might not like it at night, but we've built a close relationship with these guys and we feel like they're your best friend, almost."

One of the challenges Heitmann wrestles with is responding to customer input, which is about as varied as customers are. It's reasonable to think that an operation as big as Saputo's Waupun plant might not respond to customer requests, but Heitmann says that feedback is key to his operation. "A lot of what we do is commodity cheese and it doesn't end up on the table," he says. "I have to know: Are you going to slice this cheese, or are you going to shred it? Chunk it up, and retail a lot of it? I have to know what they're going to do with it so I can come up with the right recipe in the plant so I can meet the customer's needs."

Some combination of the plant's mammoth size, responsiveness to customers, and world-class cheese has sparked curiosity about its inner workings, something that never ceases to amaze DeMaa. "Through the years here, I can't tell you how many phone calls we've gotten from people just wanting to know what we do here," says DeMaa. "People calling from all over the country. . . . There's a lot more interest out there than I thought."

From DeMaa's perspective, there's nothing surprising about this. "You know, you'll never find a better cheese than what we make in this plant," he says. "The world championships that we've won . . . Kurt and I walk off the line and we grab a block—there's nothing special we do for that block we do for contests. It's because of the milk, the people, the equipment."

Jeff Mattes

Formerly of SARTORI FOODS, Plymouth, Wisconsin
http://www.sartorifoods.com/

Master of parmesan, romano, asiago, and fontina

We have such a rich history in Wisconsin. I felt honored to be working with my parents and my grandfather.

JEFF MATTES IS A CLASSIC WISCONSIN CHEESEMAKER—a long family history in the business led him to pursue it as his profession. "When my parents brought me home from the hospital, my first home was the second floor of our family-owned cheese factory, which my grandfather and father owned at the time up in Collins, Wisconsin," he says. "And it was said at the time, if you didn't like the factory that you worked at, you were within walking distance of another cheese factory."

Master cheesemaker Jeff Mattes is at the far right in this photo of Fairview Cheese Factory in Collins, Wisconsin, circa 1976. Others (from left to right) are his grandfather Roland "RW" Mattes; Jeff's parents, Ken and Laverne Mattes; and his brother, James Mattes. At the time of the photo, RW was seventy-five, and he remained actively involved in making cheese at the factory until his death several months later. (courtesy of Jeff Mattes)

That era has long since ended, with the consolidation of small factories and the entrance onto the scene of large corporate cheesemakers with a less direct connection to the farms and people who make the cheese. "Cheesemaking went from taking the time to ensure that the cheese had reached its optimum stage of cheese development to making 'cheese by the clock,'" Mattes observes.

Most recently, Mattes worked at the Sartori Foods plant in Plymouth, making Italian-style cheeses for more than twenty years. His background in cheesemaking, however, goes back further still.

"As we grew up, I started working for my parents during the summer when I was in fifth or sixth grade," he says. "You just matured from that, and literally right out of high school I started working for my dad and grandfather. We made cheese seven days a week."

Mattes says that cheesemaking has shifted fundamentally since his early days in the business, evolving from a time when the making of cheese was an art, first and foremost. "We did things by the seat of our pants back then," he says. "Now it's become more of a scientific thing. The science of cheesemaking is more integrated into cheesemaking. You still have the artisan part, but it's more scientific now."

Parmesan is a cheese Mattes knows intimately. "A good parmesan should have a good nutty flavor with some fruit background—you don't want a burnt flavor, but a roasted nutty flavor," he says. "Slightly fruity. It's the nutty caramelized flavor you're looking for."

Aging parmesan is an art unto itself; good aged parm has a clean, elegant flavor profile, while poorly aged parm can pick up imperfections in the body or a rank off-note. "With a good parmesan, to age it out to nine months, you need to know that the cheese is on track," says Mattes. "If something unfortunate does happen, you've got a hole in your inventory."

Another of Mattes's many hats is that of mentor. In his spare time, he referees JV and varsity football and basketball games; he has also spent many hours tutoring aspiring and midcareer cheesemakers. "I've been helping one of our cheesemakers who's been making cheese for a little more than ten years, who's going through the master cheesemaker program," says Mattes.

A lifetime of cheesemaking has made Mattes aware of Wisconsin's unique place in the industry, and more than a little proud of the state's cheese.

Jeff Mattes and a finishing table full of curd.

"I was at a cheese contest last year where one of the judges was from the state of Utah. He said he had been to a number of cheese contests in California and the cheeses were just horrible out there," Mattes says. "Everybody knows when you go to Wisconsin Badger games, you've got that song the band plays that says, 'When you've said Wisconsin, you've said it all.' Same thing can be said for Wisconsin cheeses. When you've said Wisconsin cheese, you have said it all."

The old curd cutters in Henning's Wisconsin Cheese factory in Kiel.

Ken Nett

CEDAR VALLEY CHEESE, Random Lake, Wisconsin
http://www.cedarvalleycheesestore.com/

Master of parmesan

When I was fourteen years old, I started high school, in September of '59,
and I started working in the cheese factory for a buck an hour.

LOG MORE THAN THREE DECADES in any given profession, and
you'd better take some pride in it—that's a good chunk of your life.
Ken Nett of Cedar Valley Cheese isn't short on pride in his work,
and he views the master cheesemaker program as a chance to cap
a meaningful career.

"To me, going through the program was like a football player
getting a Super Bowl ring," he says. "I was proud to do it and
happy to do it, and I brag it up whenever I can. I made cheese
for over thirty-five years, but lacked an understanding of some of
the technical aspects of cheesemaking." Nett credits Ken Sampson
of Sartori Foods with steering him toward the program. "You
take the classes and you learn the background—you understand,
after you've done it for how many years, finally what exactly was
going on."

Nett's experience means that he's got a particularly acute
understanding of how things have changed in the industry over
the years. Most central, he maintains, is the quality of milk.

Ken Nett works side by side
with his son at Cedar Valley Cheese.

"Today, you're almost guaranteed a quality milk supply. In those days, a farmer would treat a cow with penicillin, and while it wasn't legal to ship that milk—you didn't know, you had no way of checking it. And for some farmers, it was 'milk in the tank, money in the bank.'" As farmers lacked ready methods to check milk, and with an incentive to ship, quality and safety sometimes suffered. "You knew when you were making the cheese and all of a sudden your acid stopped and your pH didn't drop, and you'd say, 'Oh, here we go.' You knew you had a problem and it was too late."

Starter culture, he recalls, used to be stored in a regular gallon jug. "Nowadays, you do this, you'd think it'd be impossible to make cheese that way," he says with a laugh. "The day before, you'd catch a gallon jug of finished starter out of the starter kettle, put it in the refrigerator, and the next day you'd inoculate the new batch of sterilized whey and in about eight hours you had starter ready to make cheese. Believe it or not," he adds, "you could adjust the way your cheese was developing by adjusting that temperature to balance your rod and coccus [bacteria]."

String cheese from Cedar Valley Cheese.
Ken Nett makes string and other types of
Italian-style cheese.

Cheesemaking has become increasingly standardized. Nett tells the story of working at an Italian cheese company and being sent around to find parmesan wheels to buy. The company was concerned about quality and wanted to make sure that their source was following the same standards they'd developed in-house.

"I looked at a number of plants, and we wanted them to try to make cheese the way we did," he says. "Well, it turns out they already did. I think when you have a process, and you keep working at it to make it more efficient, and as quality controlled as you can, we all ended up at the same place. You're going out there to teach them how you make the cheese, and it turns out they're doing almost the same thing you were."

These days, Nett works a relaxing thirty-hour week at Cedar Valley Cheese, a plant that overwhelmingly produces mozzarella cheese. He appreciates the less hectic pace of work, but he particularly enjoys the opportunity to work side by side with his son Jeff. "We have a lot of good people here, but if I had to pick one person to work with, it would be my son," he says. "Not because he's my son, but because he's good to work with. He's a team player. Some people think: 'That's my job, and that's your job, and never the two shall meet,' but there are times when this guy could use some help and you know each other's jobs, and you can switch back and forth."

Nett says that the work ethic embraced by his son and himself is more than an attitude; it's something that's literally part of who they are. "It has to be in your blood," he says. "In farming, most of farming is handed down from generation to generation, so you grow into it. Here [in cheesemaking], it's to some extent the same thing."

Future generations of Netts are already enjoying the fruits of his labor. "I got a little four-year-old grandson," he says. "My wife and I will babysit for him, and the first thing he does when he comes over is look in the refrigerator for some string cheese. And he's a professional eater, too. He peels it all off. Ours is really stringy, and he gets a real kick out of it."

Annabelle the cow in Plymouth, Wisconsin.

Kerry Henning

HENNING'S WISCONSIN CHEESE, Kiel, Wisconsin
http://www.henningscheese.com/

Master of cheddar, colby, and monterey jack

We get asked, "Who does all your R & D?" Well, you're pretty much looking at it.

IF THERE EVER COMES A TIME IN LIFE—a birthday, a graduation, the launching of a major cruise ship—when you need to purchase a six-ton wheel of cheddar cheese, the good people at Henning's Wisconsin Cheese should be first on your list. Those in the know understand that master cheesemaker Kerry Henning is up to some remarkable things involving flavored and fruit-laced cheeses, but it's hard to get past the fact he also makes individual wheels on a scale that is awe inspiring, if not actually fear inducing.

One of his best known exploits took place in 2006, timed to the opening of a Central Market grocery store in Texas.

"Well, you know in Texas you have to do everything bigger," says Henning. "There's this small chain of upscale stores and they're always buying these thousand-pound wheels from us. When a store orders a big wheel of cheese, I'm always a little afraid: are they going to be able to handle this? Making a wheel of cheese that big is a tall order, but moving, cutting, wrapping, and selling a wheel that big is an even bigger feat. But when Central Market ordered a twelve-thousand-pound wheel, I thought, 'OK, these guys will be OK with it. They know how to deal with it. Their employees are trained . . . it'll be a lot more work, but they can handle it.'"

The first item to consider when ordering a six-ton wheel: logistics.

> ### TASTING NOTES: PEPPERCORN CHEDDAR
>
> The texture of peppercorn cheese is almost like that of an Italian aged cheese—a little toward the crumbly side but still sliceable. The peppercorns make the cheese merge toward the taste of aged cheddar, so it is less like getting little fireworks of pepper and more like one consistent flavor—not too peppery, but with a nice edge.

"They first ordered it, and I said, 'Are you sure your dock can handle it? It's going to be seven feet across, seven feet high. Can you roll it into your store?' They said, 'Sure, no problem.' Then one of their sister stores found out about it and said, 'If they're going to have one, we want one!' So we spaced them out about a month apart."

Mammoth cheddar cheese boxes at Henning's Wisconsin Cheese.

One of Central Market's executives came up to Kiel to get involved in the process of making the cheese, which ultimately stretched out to about forty-five days, including time to cool the cheese down and get it waxed and boxed. Then, the massive cheese went to Oshkosh for about six months of aging before being shipped to Texas.

"So it gets down there, and they're like, 'We can't get this off the truck here! Our dock won't handle this. Well, now what?'" Henning says. "They had to hire a crane company to lift it off the trailer and set it onto the concrete of their parking lot. Then they had to take out the front wall of the store where the glass is and two cash register aisles to wheel this thing into the store. Both stores had to do this! The second store was at least prepped with a forklift and they had the glass out of the way."

Kerry Henning stands by his plant's vacuum chamber.

The second store, in Dallas, had hired a sculptor to embellish the natural beauty of the massive cheese.

"She had put the school mascot, which was a dragon, into the wheel," Henning recalls. "She took the tail and wrapped it around the whole cheese. And put Dallas Cowboy football helmets into it—it was football season. . . . And then at the grand opening they had the high school band marching through the store—it was a hoot. The traffic and the shoppers were just crazy—it was almost gridlocked with carts. At times, and especially around our twelve-thousand-pounder, it was just absolute gridlock."

When Henning isn't making enormous cheeses—which sold for about $2.30 a pound in early 2008, or roughly $27,000 for a six-ton wheel—he's often playing around with new flavors and fruit/nut additives for his cheese.

"You should have been here yesterday. It smelled really good!" he says. "We were doing some cranberries and some blueberries. . . . They're fairly new yet; I'm trying to improve on the flavor of them. They're almost in the line of what I'd call a dessert cheese. Even though they're cheddar based. . . . You wouldn't eat it with a piece of bread."

Anyone can—and has—stuck fruit and other bits of food into cheese. Henning is obsessed with doing it right. "Part of the cheesemaking process is that we're converting the lactose, the sugars in the milk, to lactic acid," he says. "It's important for good-quality cheese that most of the lactose is converted during the make process. What are we doing when we start throwing in fruit? We're throwing sugar back into the recipe. We've used up all the sugar, but now we get into the problem of reintroducing sugar in what was a stable cheese. Now the bacteria can start growing again, and the quality of your cheese can start heading south and getting crumbly."

The trick is finding the right balance. "So you can add some fruit, but you don't want to add too much. But then you find out if you don't add enough fruit, there's no flavor. And if there's no flavor, then why buy it?"

Old sign in Dacada, near Random Lake.

The process of playing with flavor compounds and aging cheeses to test how the flavor changes with time can be exhausting, and each trial of a new blend can take months at a time. But Henning is committed to finding the right recipes, as exemplified by his (ultimately successful) fourteen-year effort to perfect his peppercorn cheddar, which won a bronze medal at the World Championship Cheese Contest. But now that he's fought the battle to make the best cheese, the next hurdle to overcome is production space.

"It takes up tremendous amounts of space to do this shelf curing, and we're not sure if we want to make this commitment," Henning says. "The cheese is a minimum of five months old, six months old before it leaves here, so we'd need to expand our aging program considerably to do this cheese in volume. It's one of these things you just need to do in small steps.

"So I need to introduce this cheese to a [grocery] chain that can be forgiving—you might run me out of supply real quick, but then you have to wait six months. McDonald's gets away with it with their mint shakes [available only around St. Patrick's Day], but most of the time the stores always want to have it in stock."

If Henning seems comfortable with all the aspects of the cheese business, it's a matter of nurture as much as nature. "I grew up in the business," he says. "I remember my grandfather being there, and then my father taking over when my grandfather passed away. I was snitching curds from the vat as soon as I was tall enough to reach them."

Henning's emphasis on hands-on making and old-fashioned puttering around with the cheese hearkens back to an earlier era. "Our make procedures haven't changed that much since Grandpa had the business," he says. "We've stayed backward so long we're in vogue again!"

The Masters

OF NORTHEASTERN WISCONSIN

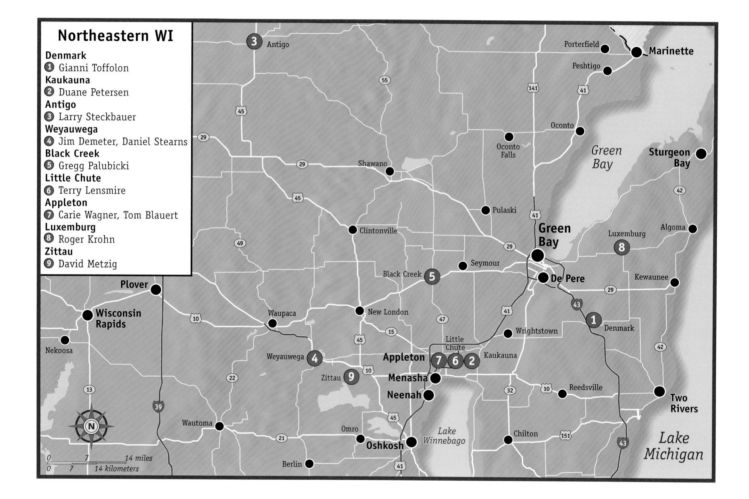

Northeastern WI

Denmark
① Gianni Toffolon
Kaukauna
② Duane Petersen
Antigo
③ Larry Steckbauer
Weyauwega
④ Jim Demeter, Daniel Stearns
Black Creek
⑤ Gregg Palubicki
Little Chute
⑥ Terry Lensmire
Appleton
⑦ Carie Wagner, Tom Blauert
Luxemburg
⑧ Roger Krohn
Zittau
⑨ David Metzig

*In seeking to duplicate the old world environment, [cheesemaker Pasquale] Frigo wrote to the
University of Wisconsin inquiring as to what area of the United States most matched Northern Italy's
summer climate. The word came back, "Go to Northern Wisconsin, young man!" And he, among other
stalwart pioneers, began the great domestic Italian cheese industry of Wisconsin.*

—RALPH SELITZER, *The Dairy Industry in America*

Northeastern Wisconsin is home to the heart-wrenchingly lovely shoreline of Door County, the seemingly
endless suburban sprawl of the Fox Valley, and—of course—Lambeau Field and the Green Bay Packers. It's
also one of Wisconsin's cheesemaking hot spots. Nine master cheesemakers work within an hour's drive of
Green Bay, and a tenth, Larry Steckbauer, works in Antigo.

Of Antigo, the *WPA Guide to Wisconsin* (1941) notes: "The Kraft-Phoenix processed-cheese factory here is
one of the largest of its kind. A cooperative creamery founded in 1930 has 900 members and has a capacity
to handle 200,000 pounds of milk daily; there is also . . . a State-supervised cooperative maple syrup
evaporating plant."

Mammoth Cheddar

The industrial scale so typical of this part of the state reached what may be its ultimate expression in 1964, when the Borden
Company sponsored the manufacture of a 34,591-pound cheddar cheese for the New York World's Fair. It was made by
Steve's Cheese of Denmark, Wisconsin, a company owned by Steve Siudzinski, and took about thirty-two hours of continuous
manufacture involving a crew of twenty-five men working in shifts. The cheese toured state fairs in a specially designed semitrailer
before going to the big show. The trailer, containing a polystyrene replica of the cheese, ended up next to Chatty Belle, the world's
largest talking cow, in Neillsville, some 170 miles west of Denmark. In 2005 a collector bought the trailer but had no interest in
the massive cheese replica. Its whereabouts are unknown. The record was surpassed in 1988 by Simon's Specialty Cheese in
Little Chute, Wisconsin (40,060 pounds), and again in 1995 by Agropur of Granby, Quebec (57,518).

Traveling through the area in the early spring of 2008, the authors encountered a Wisconsin snowstorm, several excellent family-owned butchers, and—attached to trees and marked with blue plastic bags—a still-formidable maple syruping operation in progress.

Italian cheese is particularly prominent in northeastern Wisconsin. Talking about his company's Italico cheese on the Cheese Underground blog, BelGioioso cheesemaker Mauro Rizzi said, "You need exceptionally good, clean milk to make this cheese. It must be fresh with low acidity, and Wisconsin's climate is perfect to produce the milk needed—very similar to the climate in Northern Italy."

The European influence on Wisconsin is detectable in all parts of the state, but the Continent's impact can be felt particularly in the northeast's place-names. In one morning, we drove through Holland, Denmark, and Luxemburg. Northern Europe's work ethic and stripped-down aesthetic is visible everywhere you look, from the big box stores that dot the Fox Valley's landscape to the mills, factories, and railroad connections that crowd Green Bay.

Some of the state's biggest cheesemakers call this part of the state home. Foremost Farms USA has a giant plant in Appleton, and the Trega Foods (owned by Agropur) plants produce large quantities in Weyauwega, Little Chute, and Luxemburg. Massive Saputo, too, owns plants within the region. Sartori Foods and BelGioioso Cheese, Italian artisan makers who are also no slackers when it comes to volume, call the northeast home as well, as does the local incarnation of the European giant Arla Foods.

The little guy on the block, David Metzig, couldn't be any more distinct from his corporate brethren, at least in terms of lifestyle—he still lives above his plant in tiny Zittau, Wisconsin.

Daniel Stearns and Jim Demeter stand in a cooling room surrounded by blocks of cheddar in "640" boxes. The two cheesemakers work together in two connected plants.

Gianni Toffolon

BELGIOIOSO CHEESE, Denmark, Wisconsin
http://www.belgioioso.com/

Master of parmesan and fontina

You must cultivate a group of young cheesemakers who are eager to learn like you are,
who are eager to say, "I made the cheese."

ENGLISH IS NOT MASTER CHEESEMAKER Gianni Toffolon's first
language—he came to America from Italy in 1979 to help establish a
U.S.-based Italian cheese business. Despite this, there may be no one
else in the state of Wisconsin who can so clearly and passionately
articulate the way that a committed cheesemaker feels about his work.

Toffolon got his start at a cheese-aging warehouse in Cremona,
Italy, and circumstances led to his being transferred to the cheese
factory itself.

"Right away, I fell in love with it," he says. "The milk—of course,
keep in mind I was doing very humble jobs when I was doing my
work in the cheese factory. It's not like they say, 'Here is the milk,
make the cheese.' It was more like cleaning, you know. . . . I could
see—little by little they brought me in to do more cheese-related jobs.
For example, taking the curd and stretching it. At that particular plant
we were making provolone, so there was a lot of manual labor."

Toffolon recalls the work with real affection. "You take the curd,
and then you stretch it in the hot water, and then you shape it by
hand, and then you cool it and brine it," he says. "For me, it was
fascinating—you take something as simple as milk. . . . For me,
milk was something you drink or use for breakfast in the morning.

Gianni Toffolon.

It seemed that the process of turning it into a wonderful piece of cheese . . . I said, 'This is nice.'"

Toffolon was soon working with senior cheesemakers at the plant, people who had learned the art from their fathers or grandfathers. "They were really skilled people, really intelligent, a ton of experience," he recalls. "They may not have known all the components of milk, or why you do something . . ." Here he assumes a gruff voice: "'Oh! That's because . . . you do it because it's the right thing to do!'" Old masters, Toffolon recalled, had what they called secrets. But, he notes, "Anybody that acquires that much knowledge acquires the same secrets, because your understanding of what you're doing becomes higher and higher."

Working with masters made a big impression upon the young Toffolon, and he decided to follow in their footsteps. "Just watching these people and their art and their understanding of things was amazing to me," he says. "I definitely realized at that point it was not just a job, it was an art. You're taking a growing ingredient and you're able to turn it into something that is so wonderful. It's like a mason, you know, who takes simple bricks and makes beautiful things. At that

An aging warehouse for American Grana cheese in Pulaski. The parmesan-style cheese is one of Gianni Toffolon's personal projects.

point I decided, I don't just want a job, I want something that I can put my input in it, something I can make a difference, something I can call my own. And making cheese for me was that. That was the start."

The company for which Toffolon worked had its eye on the domestic market in the United States, and was looking for ways to circumvent cheese quotas that prevented them from exporting at high quantities. The answer: open a plant in America.

"A couple of the partners were sent over here, and they looked around New York," he recalls. "They might have made a vat or two there. Then they came to Wisconsin. And they found a small cheese factory that had

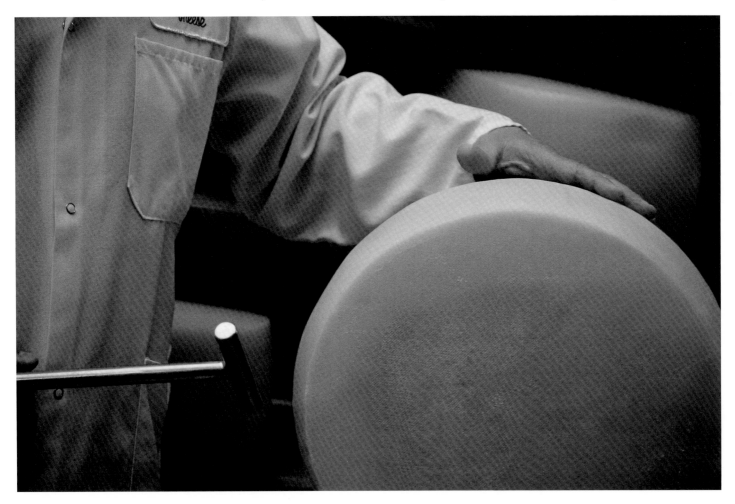

Gianni Toffolon demonstrates the grading of aged parmesan.

been abandoned, and that's where they started. So then in Italy they were looking for people who wanted to come over here."

Toffolon's life changed one evening when he was finishing up in the factory, and the owner strolled through on a tour of the plant. "He walks by me and all of a sudden he turns around and walks back and he says, 'How would you like to go to America?' I said, 'Well, uh, can I think about it?' He said, 'You have three days. On Saturday you have to leave if you want to go.' And that's how it happened."

Toffolon had been singled out as a hard worker—his spirit was just what the company needed, it had been decided, to expand into a big new territory. "They knew at that point I was committed, and they wanted someone young who was committed to the venture," he recalls. "I was twenty-three years at that time. Twenty-three years old, and you're looking at the world saying, 'I want to conquer this.'"

American Grana cheese made
by BelGioioso.

Toffolon headed over to the United States with little more than the address of the Wisconsin cheese plant and a bit of cash, but he was soon in the mix, helping the plant struggle to reinvent its product on a new continent. "When we came over, we brought the technology and knowledge of Italy," he recalls. "This company I was working for in Italy was a hundred years old, so they had a lot of tradition. So when we came over here, we said, 'In order to make great cheese, we just have to make it the same way we do in Italy.'"

It was a great plan, but it didn't work. Wisconsin milk and Italian milk are two different things entirely. "Initially the cheeses we were making were not on par with the Italian ones, and also they were not what the customer wanted over here," he says. "So even though they were good, it was neither Italian cheese nor the one the American consumer expected. So we had to humble ourselves, and say, 'The tradition doesn't work here, so we need to think how to achieve something the consumers will like while keeping as much as possible our tradition.'"

BelGioioso Cheese has since gone on to win a slew of cheese awards for everything from fresh mozzarella to provolone to mascarpone and American Grana, its own special brand of aged parmesan. A tasting of cheeses presided over by Toffolon revealed an incredible scope of products, with one consistent attribute shared by all: quality. It's something that Toffolon concentrates on—

in a strategic way—as BelGioioso's production manager.

"I spend a lot of time with the building of new locations," he says. "I guess I'm in a unique position, having grown into the cheesemaking and understanding what the cheese requires, I can now make the decision: 'For the cheese, it's better if we do this,' in terms of the building, the equipment, or the new technologies we want to use."

But the big projects sometimes get in the way of his job's small pleasures. "When we do major projects it takes me a little away from the cheese itself," he says. "But as soon as it's done—wssht!—I'm back to the cheese," he adds with a laugh. "I go back to the cheese. I really really enjoy working on the vats and finishing tables. I'm happy when I can do that—it's not work."

TASTING NOTES: CRESCENZA-STRACCHINO

Crescenza-stracchino is based on a seasonal cheese from Northern Italy. "Stracchino" alludes to the tired (or *stracca*) cows after they travel up and down the mountains.

The taste is best explained as a cross between a fresh buttermilk and a mild brie. The buttermilk flavor is a key player, and the texture stays almost liquid, but the mild brie flavor mellows the acidity and makes for a very refreshing cheese.

This cheese is a real tableside winner. Put it on a cheese plate as a counterpoint to aged flavors, or just serve it on crackers as a snack. Or sneak all that you can onto every piece of left-over baguette you can find.

Crescenza-stracchino cheese made by BelGioioso.

Duane Petersen

Arla Foods USA, Kaukauna, Wisconsin
http://www.arlafoodsusa.com/

Master of gouda and edam

I know there's room for a lot of specialty cheeses in Wisconsin and that's the area to grow.

NOT FAR FROM APPLETON—southwest of Green Bay and northeast of Lake Winnebago—lies a little slice of Europe. In 2006 the Denmark-based dairy giant Arla Foods USA purchased White Clover Dairy, a sprawling, century-old plant known for its premium edam and gouda cheeses. And while European management may run the strategic picture, it's a local boy who oversees the cheese.

"Originally, I grew up in the country," says master cheesemaker Duane Petersen. Along with his older brother, Petersen got a job at a factory just south of De Pere, where the intensity of workdays was measured in quarts of sweat. "The first years, everything was labor intensive. You'd do a lot of cheddaring, if you're familiar with that process," he says, referring to the cutting, lifting, and stacking of whey-saturated curds often described as backbreaking.

"That's the way it was done," Petersen says, matter-of-factly. "Every plant was the same. You'd put your curd and whey on a table, drain the whey off, and end up with a big long cheese pack. You'd cut it and you'd turn it, and turn it, and turn it. . . . Pretty soon you get slabs that are about that thick [puts fingers close together] and weigh sixty pounds. You're bent over a table, and you're throwin' 'em. And then you throw them through a mill. One vat is about thirty-five-hundred pounds. You'd pick every piece up and you'd run it through there. You'd do eighteen of those a day." He pauses for a second, remembering, amused. "There were some pretty big boys walking around here. It was hard work. Hot. You didn't have air-conditioning and air movement like plants nowadays. It was, well, if you could open a window when the state inspectors weren't around, you would."

Along with increasing automation and the blessing of air-conditioning, the modern era has brought a Continental style of management to the Arla-owned plant. "They have a really good handle on how to run their business, what's important, what's not important. They do take care of their people, and they really stress that. And a lot of it is more where the person has to help himself work through the company. They're always trying

120

to educate people—they have a program [for employee training], and that all has to do with how you do your job and how you direct yourself toward your employees. And communication—it's a little different than what I was used to."

That translates to a workplace where employees can be frank with management. "They want your input," Petersen says. "They're real informal on that. If you're going to have a meeting with your management, there's no holds barred; you say what you want to say. There's no grudges. Which is different than what I'd been dealing with."

Duane Petersen, certified in edam and gouda cheeses.

Fostered at least in part by a team that works well together, the plant puts out a European-style cheese that can be stacked up wheel to wheel against its Continental counterpart.

"We do the gouda and edam almost exactly like it's done in Holland," he says. "In fact, we've won competitions against cheese plants in Holland. I know some of the guys from the plants, and when you're in a competition like this year, you get a few jabs back and forth at each other. But we do the old traditional style—pressed under whey and made with the eye openings."

While the make processes for most cheeses call for draining off whey before pressing the curd (or letting the curd compact under its own weight), Petersen's line of work calls for a different approach.

"In a gouda-type cheese, the trick of it— you have your curd and whey, and the best thing is to not have the curd exposed to any air," Petersen says. "So you have your curd underneath your whey and it gives you a whole different body. And we use some eye developers to give you some small openings— almost like a Swiss, but they're really small. That all has to do with that being pressed under whey. The cheese stays under that until it goes into the hoop. It's like a solid block."

Yellow flowers decorate Highway 45 near Medina Junction.

Larry Steckbauer

Sʌʀᴛᴏʀɪ Fᴏᴏᴅs, Antigo, Wisconsin
http://www.sartorifoods.com/

Master of parmesan and romano

*Making parmesan cheese really hasn't changed much. And for us, that's a good thing.
The good things, you hang onto.*

Tᴏ ᴛᴇʟʟ ᴛʜᴇ sᴛᴏʀʏ ᴏғ Lᴀʀʀʏ Sᴛᴇᴄᴋʙᴀᴜᴇʀ, you have to tell the story of the plant in which he works. It's a Sartori Foods plant now, but it got its start as a Kraft cheese plant, the second owned by founder James L. Kraft. Steckbauer points out the window of his plant's conference room, into what is currently a whirling white blender of fat, wet snowflakes.

"Years ago, as you see right across the street, there was a railroad corridor between here and that stop sign," he says. "This used to be a brewery on this side of the road. On that side it used to be called the Sheboygan Creamery."

Kraft, on his way up to a summer home about twenty miles north of Antigo, decided that the brewery and creamery—both of which were up for sale—would be a good place for a cheese plant, so he bought them.

"Over the years they made a lot of different products here," says Steckbauer. "At one time it was the largest swiss cheese

Brining tanks are an integral part of the cheesemaking process at the plant that Larry Steckbauer oversees.

manufacturing facility in the world. I don't think they put out a whole lot, but back in the 1920s, it was big. They made a lot of things over the years. They made popcorn coating, they did some dabbling in baby food, and I believe it was in the 1940s they started making parmesan, to try it out."

The experiment worked—the cheese was terrific. "At that time too Kraft had—shortly after that—three plants making parmesan," Steckbauer says. "And for some reason, the cheese out of this facility was always found to be the best."

The parm train came to a screeching halt in 1993, when Philip Morris purchased Kraft. "Everything with Philip Morris was huge," Steckbauer says. "Little Antigo didn't cut it anymore." Suddenly, a perfectly good parmesan plant known for its high-quality product was doomed, victim of a massive corporation's effort to increase quantity at all costs.

"The employees really knew what kind of a product we had here, and we thought we'd be successful on our own," Steckbauer says. "So we purchased the plant from Kraft. It was not only employees putting in all their 401K money, which was pretty scary, but we also had help from the city and the state, local investors, and our patrons."

Stacks of parmesan-style cheese called SarVecchio are aged in Sartori's Antigo plant.

Kraft helped with the transition too, but the plant, then known as the Antigo Cheese Company, got off to a white-knuckle start. "There were probably eighty-some employees when we took over, and about forty or so left," Steckbauer says. "We never bad-mouthed anybody who made that decision. The ones who stuck around went through basic hell. A lot of sleepless nights. The first year was very, very tough."

The plant did all right, got to its feet again, produced some tremendously good cheese, and survived until 2006, when it was purchased by the family-run Sartori Foods. The Antigo plant contributes to the Sartori plan on the artisan side of things.

"Before they purchased us, they were not into the retail business, but now they're going into that quite heavily," he says. "It's really becoming one of their main focuses."

Key to the retail strategy is a twenty-month aged parmesan once called Stravecchio, and now rebranded (and copyrighted) as SarVecchio. People who know cheese know that it's one of the finer domestic parmesans available, and that it can stand up even to European imports.

> **TASTING NOTES: SARVECCHIO**
>
> SarVecchio is a disarmingly sweet and mellow aged parmesan–style cheese. It is slightly crumbly and rich in flavor without being acidic or overpowering. It finishes on a mild and unexpectedly creamy note.

"I'll tell you a quick story," says Steckbauer, warming to the topic of good aged parm. "I was in Minneapolis at the International Dairy-Deli-Bakery exposition a couple years ago and this guy came over to our booth. He'd just tried our parmesan and he said, 'Man, this is really good stuff. I want you to come over to my booth and taste what I have.'" Steckbauer agreed and went over to try a sample.

"He gave me a piece of it, and I thought, 'Oh, no. This is really good.' He had a big grin on his face and he said, 'You know where I got this from?' And I said no." To Steckbauer's profound relief, the man said, "Antigo Cheese" and started laughing.

To appreciate SarVecchio, it helps to try it, but Steckbauer does a pretty good job of putting its intangible quality into words. "Normal parmesan is aged ten months," he says. "As it develops, it breaks down the proteins, and short of getting real technical, that's about it. We hand-select the best parmesan and age it out. Antigo—there's something in this locality. I don't know if it's the milk, but it gives the parmesan a distinct taste."

Sweet and nutty are the two attributes Steckbauer uses to sum up the cheese. "I used to go out to shows and things like that," he says. "Other cheesemakers would say, 'Here comes the guy who makes the candy cheese.' Once you start eating it, you just really enjoy the sweetness."

Jim Demeter and Daniel Stearns

Trega Foods (Agropur), Weyauwega, Wisconsin
http://www.tregafoods.com/

Masters of feta (Demeter), cheddar (Stearns)

If the clock is telling you one thing and you feel something else, you just throw the clock out.
But once you get to the eighty thousand pounds a day, that's very difficult.
—JIM DEMETER

Jim Demeter with forms for his feta.

ASK JIM DEMETER IF HE'S EVER CONSIDERED a career other than cheesemaking, and, more likely than not, you'll get a hearty chuckle in response. "For me it never really was an option," he says. "I am a fourth generation cheesemaker—I just really grew up with it.

"Dad was a native of Greece and got over here after the war on a scholarship for agriculture," he says. "My mother [Dorothy Renter] was the only child and she did not want to go into the family business—she wanted to be a history teacher—but her dad said, 'You're going to be a cheesemaker.' She ended up going to Iowa State in Ames and was the first woman to graduate with a degree in dairy science.

"There she met my dad. Their class project was baby swiss cheese, so they were one of the first ones to work with baby swiss back in the '50s. They brought it home to Lena, Illinois, and it kind of just took off from there."

Changing times and a takeover by a large French company pushed his parents into retirement, and Demeter hit the road.

126

"It was really difficult to be a family and then go into a global corporate setting," he says. "I tried to make it fit for ten years and then I moved north."

Demeter, who oversees the production of feta at the Trega Foods plant in Weyauwega, grew up with feta in his blood. "It was a really good experience growing up with it," he says. "I started when I was fourteen years old, hand-washing feta. It was interesting to watch feta cheese grow as you started out at a vat a week, then it just slowly got bigger and bigger. When I was eighteen years old, the head cheesemaker was from Switzerland. Every summer he went back to Switzerland for a whole month, and the plant always would struggle when he was away. Then one time I got tapped to do his job and we did OK. We did pretty good," he admits. "And that's when I knew 'I think I got something.'"

As Demeter's career has evolved, so has the scope of his cheesemaking. These days, his plant leans on the strength of a coagulator, a massive belt-driven system that automates nearly every aspect of feta production. The device at Demeter's command is one of only two in the United States. "I speak just for the feta department—we run close to eighty thousand pounds [of cheese] a day," he says. "[The coagulator system] makes us

Trega Foods has four master cheesemakers. Clockwise from bottom left: Roger Krohn, Daniel Stearns, Terry Lensmire, and Jim Demeter. (courtesy of Wisconsin Milk Marketing Board)

and the Buholzers down at Klondike very special. It allows you to make the volume. I just hear these stories of how these guys used to make thirty-five to forty thousand pounds of cheese in open vats. It was a lot of work. A lot of manual labor. This takes it out and brings a consistency back in. When it works it's a work of art, but when it doesn't it's a piece of junk," he says with a laugh.

"That's been the real challenging part—being a cheesemaker and then yet trying to troubleshoot," he says. "With all of the automation there is a lot of electronics, encoders, programming—the program has to be satisfied in order to see the process work, and sometimes you have to trick it and sometimes it slaps you."

The challenge, according to Demeter, comes when dealing with a vat that's wrestling with sluggish starter. With a vat, you can give the cheese more time. With the coagulator, the belt keeps turning.

Daniel Stearns, Demeter's colleague, wrestles with similar challenges of scale and volume. But while Demeter's cheese of choice is feta, Stearns deals with cheddar— towering, 640-pound blocks of it. The automation of the plant, he says, brings with it the advantage of a consistent product.

"I think actually it is a positive route, the way we make here, because it is so consistent day to day to day," Stearns says. "We make very few adjustments on a day-to-day basis. If anything it's a seasonal change, due to the change in the milk composition. That's about it."

Although his product comes out in big quantities—the plant's storage area recalls the scene in *Raiders of the Lost Ark* where the Ark is concealed in an absurdly massive government warehouse—Stearns says volume alone isn't enough to sustain the company or the state's dairy industry as a whole. "We're the largest cheesemaking state in the country, but California and others are coming out with megaplants," he says. "But, especially our company, we thrive on quality besides quantity. I think that is going to help us last out there up against the big ones."

Large boxes of cheese known as 640s (a reference to their weight, in pounds) are transported throughout the factory on a monorail system.

The crates of cheese that dominate the line on Stearns's side of the plant conjure up images of a medieval workshop crossed with the auto-building robots of Detroit—when your mind finally wraps itself around the volume of cheese that dances across the floor, it reels. It takes ten days in a refrigeration room for one of the massive cheddar blocks to cool completely from about eight-eight degrees to forty degrees; in the meantime, Stearns ensures that each block is tested at five and ten days for fat, pH, salt, and moisture. Beyond that, a grader will taste each cheese when it hits the age of about two and a half to three months. The plant's storage capacity has decreased, but at one point, it could hold sixteen million pounds of cheese.

Stearns, for his part, looks for a well-balanced final product when he samples his cheddar. "Not too sweet, not too bitter," he says. "And besides that there is the body of the cheese. There has to be a nice clean surface, no impurities or marks on it. The color has to be very uniform."

Stearns takes the change that overtook Trega in 2008—the company's sale to Canadian food giant Agropur—in stride. "I think it is a positive thing for us," he says. "The owners wanted to retire, and the company has been well off financially. It made sense for [Agropur] to buy them out, since they wanted to expand in the U.S. market. What better way than to jump onboard this brand."

Stearns and Demeter both see a bright future for their company and for Wisconsin cheese in general. Although plants out West—in California, Idaho, and New Mexico, in particular—are doing enormous volumes, Demeter says that quality will set Wisconsin cheese apart from the competition.

"As long as they can get a certain pH and a certain moisture they call it cheese," says Demeter. "For some customers that's OK, but in the long run the quality is going to win out over quantity. We do pretty good on a volume basis, too, but basically we can do a quality job. We have the people and the knowledge. "

He could easily have added something about Wisconsin bloodlines, too—Demeter has at least one heir coming up through the ranks. "I actually have a son who is running vats on cheddar—Nathan—and I got another boy that's working a summer job too, but he doesn't know which way he's going yet. It's like *Star Wars*: 'It's your destiny,'" he adds with a laugh. "But my oldest boy, Nathan, is pretty much into it and is going to be the fifth generation."

Daniel Stearns manages the plant's cheddar operation.

Times have changed, even if the last name of the cheesemaker remains Demeter. "I try to encourage him because to do it the way I did it—the hard way—doesn't really work; it's really difficult to do it today," Demeter says. "I try to encourage him to go to school and get some kind of degree because it would be so much easier. I say, 'I can't teach you the way my dad taught me.'"

Automation is a big part of the change. "It is so different. It's learning programming, it's learning how to run machines and stuff like that. But he's really catching on. They asked him to run vats, which is a pretty big responsibility; he knows he'll get hammered if he screws up. I'm pretty proud of that."

Classic signs on a barn on Highway 52 outside of Wausau.

Gregg Palubicki

Saputo Cheese USA (formerly Alto Dairy Cooperative), Black Creek, Wisconsin
http://www.saputousafoodservice.com/alto_site4.html

Master of cheddar and colby

The longer I'm into this, the more fascinating it is.

IF THE MODERN, AUTOMATED CHEESEMAKING HAS A FACE, it may be that of Gregg Palubicki, who presides over Saputo Cheese USA's sophisticated Black Creek facility. More automated than even the sprawling Waupun facility (formerly Alto's flagship plant), Black Creek is a forest of stainless steel and silicon.

"There's goods and bads about mechanization," Palubicki says. "I think it's harder to make a good piece of cheese if you're totally mechanized and running off the clock. Bigger plants run basically off the clock. Some of these smaller guys, if you've been down to Green County—those guys can babysit a vat of cheese, and they can get whatever they want to get."

Palubicki's challenge, therefore, is to make good cheese—and a lot of it—without being able to do hands-on fine tuning. "We're kind of behind the eight ball because whatever's up in that vat we're going to get—we can't babysit because we're on the clock. We're all about, kind of, how much throughput we can get from the plant."

If awards are anything to judge by, he and his team are doing pretty well. One of the plant's colby jack cheeses won its class at the 2008 World Championship Cheese and Butter Contest. "In the last two years, we've taken four major awards," he says. "We won the state fair with it one year, we won the grand championship at the World Dairy Expo in 2006 with it. It's not like we're making a ton of it—we make one vat maybe every two months."

Credit for high quality cheese starts, he says, with good quality milk and experienced cheesemakers. "It's the milk," he says. "It's all about good milk. We're blessed in Wisconsin, especially in this area. Plus we have a lot of

---

**TASTING NOTES:
SAPUTO PASTURE-GRAZED CHEDDAR**

This one-year aged cheddar is more yellow than other uncolored cheddars; it is common for cheese made from milk of grass-fed cows to have this richer color. The flavor is buttery and smooth, with no acid flavor at all— uncommon in an aged cheddar. It has a soft and creamy texture.

Gregg Palubicki dons gloves to test the curd.

experienced cheesemakers in this plant," he adds. "There isn't a lot of experience out there these days, but we're blessed with guys that have been making cheese for twenty-five years."

The skill of his veteran cheesemakers and the relative lack of people to replace them are among Palubicki's greatest concerns for the future of cheesemaking in Wisconsin. "Even with the automation, my whole fear is that people are just going to be pushing buttons, and they don't know why they're pushing the buttons," he says. "Here we've got guys who know why they're pushing the buttons. But whenever we try to hire somebody, there isn't somebody that's experienced anymore."

His respect for experience appears to be a family trait. His father started work at the plant in 1959 and retired in 2000, having served as plant manager at one point. "I can remember him getting up at all odd hours of the day, and coming home at eleven o'clock in the morning," he says. "Then he'd sleep all day and you'd hardly see him. I used to come down with him—I found it kind of interesting."

The spark of interest was soon kindled into an exhausting but rewarding high school job. "I started working part time before school," he says. "So I'd get up at four o'clock in the morning and come to work before school. I'd work from four to eight, take a shower, and go to school, sleep through my first class. . . . That's how I started. I can't thank him enough—he had a great work ethic. He wasn't afraid to put in seventy or eighty hours a week. I try not to do that, but . . . he was [and still is] an impressive man."

Palubicki's start coincided with an era of consolidation that reshaped the Wisconsin dairy industry. "Back when I started, that's when a lot of those small factories were closing down," he says. "And the cheesemakers from those places were coming to places like this. I got to work with a lot of those guys, and they all had different ideas. I thought it was fascinating. One guy would think he had the right recipe, and then the next guy—it was constant bickering between these guys when they'd work together."

Deep roots in Wisconsin cheese allowed Palubicki and his team to take some risks; in 2006 Alto launched a line of pasture-grazed cheeses. Not surprising for an artisan plant. But to quote the blog Cheese Underground: "For those of us born in Wisconsin and raised on Velveeta, this is huge. THE biggest cooperative in Wisconsin is now making a pasture-grazed cheese."

"You can taste the difference, and you can see the difference," Palubicki says. "If you take a piece of this white cheddar, and you compare it to pasture-grazed, that pasture-grazed would have a golden hue to it because of the feed. Also, the flavor is more . . . kind of more earthy and more full, cheesy flavor."

If Palubicki's past is any indication, he'll keep innovating until he calls it quits. "I've been making cheese for thirty-odd years, and you tend to learn something every day," he says. "I don't know how many jobs you can really do that at. Did I ever think this would be my career? No. But it just happened, and I'm happy with it."

Terry Lensmire

TREGA FOODS (Agropur), Little Chute, Wisconsin
http://www.tregafoods.com/

Master of cheddar, monterey jack, mozzarella, and provolone

I guess the cheese was in the blood, is probably the best way to put it.

Master cheesemaker Terry Lensmire
of Trega Foods.

QUITE A FEW OF THE STATE'S MASTER CHEESEMAKERS have deep roots in the industry. But not only are Terry Lensmire's roots deep—three generations deep, to be precise—they're also broad.

"My grandfather actually worked for three or four cheese plants in his life," he says. "He also had several brothers that were cheesemakers at the time, as did my dad, who had two brothers that were cheesemakers, and at one time that I can remember there were five different families of Lensmires that had cheese plants or were associated with cheese plants. Pretty much all in eastern Wisconsin." And although Lensmire's father worked at three different plants over the course of his life, he spent the bulk of his time working for his own dad.

Family history isn't necessarily destiny, and Lensmire—a trumpet player who's part of the University of Wisconsin–Manitowoc Lakeshore Wind Ensemble—hasn't always been fully in thrall to cheese.

"I actually have a degree in music education," he says. "I taught for three and a half years, but all the while I was teaching I was grading cheese for a company also. But as I look back, there was maybe one year since I became a teenager that I didn't have some involvement in dairy or cheese industry." Those teaching skills haven't been wasted at the plant, where Terry, like many masters, is able to pass his knowledge on to a new generation. The soft skills that you hone as a teacher—

communication, team building, maintaining order amid chaos—are in many ways equally applicable in a cheese plant.

Working at Trega Foods (now owned by Agropur) in Little Chute, Luxemburg, and Weyauwega, Lensmire spends much of his time on the development of new products, working with cheese and whey products. The emphasis on the customer, he says, has become increasingly critical. "When I worked for my grandfather and father, you made cheddar cheese, you made colby cheese," he says. "Now you may make cheddar cheese that has a specific attribute to meet the customer expectations or you may make a mozzarella that has no stretch to it, or super stretch to it, or no browning."

The finishing tables of the Trega Foods plant in Luxemburg, Wisconsin.

That new emphasis has helped to turn Lensmire from a cheesemaker into a cheesemaking technician, able to finely tune the various attributes of his products to meet specific demands. "Customers are more, I will use the word 'demanding,' about the product they want. So now the industry has become much more focused on 'I don't only make cheddar, I make cheddar for this application.'"

The first step, he says, is understanding the customer's needs, a process that typically begins by obtaining a sample similar to what the customer is looking for. "We take that sample and apply it to the application they want to use it in and we see the body of the cheese—does it stretch, is it firm, is it soft, no stretch, melt, no melt? Look at the flavor: Are there dairy notes? What kinds of flavors are in the cheese? That is our starting point."

From there, it's a matter of considering existing cheeses to see how—or if—the make can be modified to suit the customer's request. Meeting new challenges on a regular basis is something Lensmire says can be accomplished only through the constant acquisition of new knowledge.

"I think one of the things we will all say is that we never stop learning," he says. "It always seems there is something new out there for us to try. I think that is an important thing in the heritage of the Wisconsin master cheesemaker. We are not old guys, but we have been at it for a long time. And every one of these people always feels there is more they can learn."

Lensmire was in the first class of master cheesemakers to graduate, in 1997. "The program was being developed," he says, "and I inquired about it. What do you have to do? And they said, 'Oh, we don't know yet.'"

Lensmire sees the future of Wisconsin cheesemaking going in the direction of the master program: expertly trained makers who are capable of feats of artistry, not simply industry. "I don't think Wisconsin will be a mass cheese producer anymore, a commodity type cheese producer," he says. "I think we will be making more specialized products from now on. And I think that is where the master cheesemaker program has helped that part of the cheesemaking."

Carie Wagner and Tom Blauert

Foremost Farms USA, Various plants (Wagner), Appleton, Wisconsin (Blauert)
http://www.foremostfarms.com/

Masters of havarti, asadero, cheddar, and monterey jack (Wagner), mozzarella and low-fat mozzarella (Blauert)

Of all the things I've worked with, I've always been pretty passionate about cheesemaking.
—CARIE WAGNER

EVERY PIECE OF CHEESE HAS A STORY BEHIND IT. Each wheel, wedge, block, or bag of shreds is the end product of labor, microfauna, marketing plans, purchasing agreements, distribution networks, R & D, and good old-fashioned milk.

As much as—or more than—any other master cheesemaker, Carie Wagner has seen every facet of the big picture. At this point (in a career that has encompassed hands-on cheesemaking, R & D, and quality control), she currently works in purchasing at Foremost Farms USA. As cheese producers go, Foremost is a respectable size. "We produce about five hundred million pounds of cheese a year," she says. "Which means we're taking in . . . about five billion pounds of milk. We have plants that take a million pounds of milk a day alone."

Wagner's dairy science and corporate background is built upon a lifetime of dairy knowledge—like many of her master cheesemaker peers, she's known cows all her life. "My parents still milk cattle," she says. "I was really close to both sets of grandparents. They were kind of this old German self-sufficient farm. They had cattle, they raised a lot

Tom Blauert in front of the whey factory of the Foremost Farms USA plant in Appleton.

Carie Wagner grades a piece of Foremost Farms cheddar.

of dogs, poultry, a lot of hogs, so not only did they milk, but they processed all their meat and made a lot of sausages. We grew up with things kids won't eat today—blood sausage and veal sausage."

When her parents had to take jobs off the farm, Wagner actually ran the family farm in high school. At the urging of her parents, she went to college at the University of Wisconsin–River Falls.

"I put myself through school, and that's actually how I got into making cheese," she says. While attending River Falls, Wagner—leader of the food science club—helped set up the school's dairy plant as one of the first two student managers.

"We had a vat that didn't have an agitator on it, so we actually hand stirred," she says, a little ruefully. "We had a little bulk tank on a trailer, and I would drive the truck up to the farm. I remember backing in, filling it up with milk, backing it up into these doors. . . . Thinking back, I was pretty fearless back then. Or just stupid," she adds with a laugh.

The small-scale making at the dairy plant proved to be the foundation of a long career in cheesemaking. "I just kind of did the whole process," she says. "I don't think the vat that didn't have agitation lasted very long because it wasn't a good use of our work, but it did give you an appreciation for stirring, and good upper body strength. But we hand cut, and we did stuff more on a small scale so we could see what was going on."

The chief of the University of Wisconsin–River Falls plant, Renee May, brought Wagner into the world of cheesemaking with a combination of warmth and persistence. "She's patient. I always had trouble putting the homogenizer together, and she'd bend down beside you and say things go this way, things go that way," Wagner says. "We always had a lot of fun in our class, and you just learned and grew so much and so smoothly that you didn't even know it was happening.

"Back then I didn't realize how much I was learning hands-on, day to day," she says. "I'd have to drive to Ellsworth to pick up our starter culture. I had these stainless steel pails, and I'd just take some pails of culture, put covers on them, and then bring them back and measure them out. She taught us about—as we went through their culture program—why we had more acid on this one, or why that one went faster. At the time, you're probably kind of listening, but I didn't really think I'd be making cheese after I left college."

The experience turned out to be formative. "She could have just let me go off and say, 'Yep, I made cheese.' But she said, 'Go get your license. Get some more work out of this.'" After working on butter manufacture after graduation, Wagner took a job at Kraft in Beaver Dam, a move that put her firmly in the big leagues of manufacturing; from there, she moved to Nutrasweet to make low fat cheese, working with a whey protein–based fat substitute.

"When I got back to Kraft and was making cheese again, I realized: I really, really enjoy that side of the business. I enjoyed knowing about the starter cultures, and what works better, and rotations . . . so Renee laid that really nice foundation," she says, laughing. "It was so cool out there, we had research people—I just have a bachelor's, and then I've supplemented with classes and licenses—we actually had Ph.D. people making cheese in little vats that looked like little Double-O's. One of my jobs was then upscaling those to the pilot plant where we had 500- and 1,000-pound vats and we would run stuff through. And then I would take those products and that information to customers so they could do it full scale.

"And then I met my husband," she says. "He was a research microbiologist for Kraft, so he was doing challenge studies for any new food products to make sure they were safe to eat. . . . He was doing similar work and his lab had the freezer where I had my starter cultures."

Carie Wagner.

A classic romance.

Eventually Wagner moved to Foremost Farms, which also employs master cheesemaker Tom Blauert. Blauert runs the Foremost Farms plant at Appleton, which produced a shredded cheese that took first place in its class at the 2008 World Championship Cheese Contest.

"We didn't do anything special; we just found the proper characteristics for the cheese," says Blauert, who is modest even by the standards of his soft-spoken peers. "We try to hold the line on using quality ingredients, maintaining sanitation and safety. Even though my name was on the cheese, it's not something one person can do—it's always going to be a joint effort."

Blauert describes himself as a hands-off manager who tries to "hire people smarter than I am." In his off-time, he cuts oak from his own woods and crafts gifts for the plant's office staff, including roll-top breadboxes and Amish-style wastebaskets.

Blauert credits the master cheesemaker program with helping him get a better handle on some of the technical aspects of cheesemaking. "The program helped me understand starter culture systems," he says. "A dairy works with live cultures, and the cheese is always growing and developing—you just can't stop. It's a constant process."

Both Blauert's work and Wagner's position involve dealing with variables on a scale and level of sophistication that would boggle less experienced cheesemakers. "I'm doing the starters, the rennets, the lactic acids, things like that," Wagner says. "And I'm holding our suppliers to accountability for consistency and not swapping on us."

Although purchasing is her focus, Wagner keeps a metaphorical hand in the curd. "I've always been pretty passionate about cheesemaking of all the things I've worked with. Helping people out and answering questions, I still have a lot of the plants call me and say, 'Hey, I want to get my cheese grader's license, can you help to get me situated?' Or they'll be having a pH problem. . . . I remember laughing with my dad one time over a holiday. . . . You know, I didn't want a dairy farm a couple of years after college because I saw what it was like to have free time. But if I had known a cheesemaker's schedule was as crazy as a farmer's, I would have had to rethink this whole concept.

"I like to think . . . I bring a different spin to [the master cheesemaker program] because I've worked for larger companies, not just small plants. I think about probiotics, and what are the positive things that are being brought by marketing trends . . . besides just good quality, good-tasting cheese."

Although Wagner is the only female certified master cheesemaker, she says the gender issue is typically the last thing on her mind, and her peers have welcomed her with open arms. At one particular convention, Wagner says, she made an important breakthrough with one member of the brotherhood she describes as "more traditional."

One cheesemaker event ended with a bus ride to a Brewers game in a bus full of cheesemakers. After a high-spirited reception, the beer was flowing and the cheesemakers were giving each other a hard time. One more traditional—and famously gruff—master cheesemaker suddenly turned to Wagner and said, "Wagner, you know what? You're all right. You know how to make cheese and drink beer like the rest of us.'"

"And that was my crowning moment. Funnier than heck."

A barn near Medina Junction on Highway 96.

Roger Krohn

TREGA FOODS (Agropur), Luxemburg, Wisconsin
http://www.tregafoods.com/

Master of mozzarella and provolone

There are just so many years of tradition here.

IF YOU VISIT THE CONFERENCE ROOM in Roger Krohn's cheese plant, you're immediately struck by the old photos that line the walls. It's not merely that they're old; they're generationally old, telling a continuous story that stretches back into the nineteenth century, when the plant was born. Aerial shots of the plant show its recent evolution and expansion; a hand-tinted closeup shows an early-model milk truck, with spoked tires and a buggylike hood, pulled up to the plant's small porch. A middle-aged working man in overalls and a cap stands by one of the porch beams looking skeptically at the camera.

"The plant was built in 1892," says Krohn. "It was actually my great-great-uncle who built the plant, Albert Gruetzmacher. And the guy standing on the porch is my grandfather Charles Krohn. He was the first cheesemaker at this plant. And in 1907 he purchased the plant from Albert Gruetzmacher, and a family member has worked at the plant ever since."

Although the plant has modern equipment, and is, as of 2008, part of the Canadian Agropur megadairy co-op, there are traces of the past everywhere. In the plant itself there's an old, comic mural of a talking cow standing next to a wheel of cheese. And although the original plant was mostly torn down in the early '40s, its successor, built in '44, is still part of the current plant.

"That's been added onto ever since," Krohn says. "If you look at the pictures, it's kind of progressing. When the factory turned one hundred years old in 1992, we had a big party for all of our dairy producers, and my sister did a book that has the whole history. She even has little dots on this map of Kewaunee County for all the plants; this is the only dairy plant left in the county. There used to be plants on every corner, because farmers had to bring the milk with horses to the plant."

Like so many others, the plant got its start making classic American-style cheeses, such as cheddar. But in 1960 Roger's father, Leo, made a dramatic move.

"My dad started making mozzarella in 1960," Krohn says. "That's when the pizzerias really got going, in the 1960s—there were only two in Green Bay in 1960. So that was a kind of daring move for him to do that. A lot people thought, 'Leo Krohn is crazy,' but it turned out to be a pretty good move on his part."

The mozzarella boom hasn't subsided, and it's still the plant's mainstay product. "We make enough cheese for 120,000 pizzas a day," he says. "I read somewhere that in the United States we eat a hundred acres of pizza every day, or the equivalent of 350 slices per second. Pizza's been very good for the industry, and I often wonder where we'd be without it."

Leo Krohn passed on in 1990. "He was in the plant," says Roger. "He was in his office and he just kind of fell off his chair. Everybody said it was kind of fitting because he was born in the cheese factory, and he died in the cheese factory."

Leo left a legacy behind him, however, in the make procedures that govern the plant's cheese production.

"We like to go after higher-end users on the East Coast—New York, New Jersey, Pennsylvania," Roger Krohn says. "These people are kind of from the old country and they know pizza. . . . They still make pizzas in brick ovens. They know cheese and they're willing to pay a little more for it."

What makes a good mozz? Krohn narrows it down a bit: "We don't try to enhance the yield of our cheese by adding nonfat dry milk," he says. "Not that there's anything wrong that, but it will

Roger Krohn and a portrait of his father, Leo.

affect the final performance of the cheese somewhat. We make our mozzarella the old-fashioned, Old World way of skimming cream out of the milk instead of adding nonfat solids to the milk to get to a certain fat percentage in the cheese. You can add skim milk powder or condensed skim milk. We actually remove cream to get to the fat we want."

The make procedure pays off on the back end, when a pizza or cheese maven samples the product. "Most of the really sharp pizza guys can tell," Krohn says. "And the really good cheese graders can pick up the powder flavor in the cheese itself."

The family business—known as Krohn Dairy Products—was sold to Weyauwega Milk Products in 2000, in part of a three-way merger/buyout that also involved Simon's Specialty Cheese. "In 2003, they brought them all under the Trega name," Krohn says. "*Tre* is three, and *ga* is just the end of Weyauwega, and our tagline is 'great people, great products'—if you spin the letters in our name, they spell 'great.'"

Trega Foods was bought by Canada's largest dairy co-op, Agropur, at the beginning of 2008, but despite the new ownership, Krohn is optimistic about the plant and its cheese. "We feel good about it, and that good things will happen," he says.

A cattail outside of the
BelGioioso Cheese plant in Pulaski.

David Metzig

Union Star Cheese Factory, Zittau, Wisconsin
http://www.unionstarcheese.com/

Master of cheddar

I have a lot of confidence that if we take care of quality first, we are going to be long-term successful.

David Metzig.

LIVING ABOVE YOUR CHEESE PLANT is supposed to be a historical condition, a quirk of the past when Wisconsin cheesemaking was still growing out of its origins as something that farm wives did to earn a little extra money or preserve milk for the winter months. The intimacy of hearing the clanking, rumbling, and hissing of machinery at all hours of day; the constant access to work; the ever-present reality of having to make thousands more pounds of cheese each day: these are all things that cheesemakers have sought to get away from—at least a little bit. But for David Metzig, his wife, and their ten-year-old son, making cheese is still a way of life in the most complete sense of the expression. Above the family's small plant in the unincorporated town of Zittau, Metzig's living quarters are warm and homey, appointed with country antiques and carefully crafted wooden furniture.

One of Metzig's four grown sons has stuck with the business and works for Crave Brothers Farmstead Cheese—clearly the arrangement isn't purely a recipe for cheesemaking burnout.

"I think it is a nice lifestyle actually," Metzig says. "We work so much, but we are home all the time. I am not a real private person, and that lack of privacy really bothers some people. Our kids have enjoyed it. You have some family identity."

Metzig mentions that his family's arrangement used to be very common. "I think you see the problem with working women, and how hard it is to raise a family compared to having a business in the home," he says. "It's much easier having the kids and the business together, rather than having to do daycare."

Metzig traces the origin of his Union Star Cheese Factory back to a key advance in dairy science at the turn of the nineteenth century. "In 1907, Professor [Stephen Moulton] Babcock figured out that, by adding some acid to a sample of milk, the butterfat would cook out of the milk, and then you could put it into a little flask with a long thin neck that was calibrated," he says. "At that point, you could take a little calipers and measure how deep the butterfat was in the glass."

The Babcock Test led to cheese factories paying farmers for milk with higher butterfat content. Certain breeds of cows became more valuable, but conditions got tougher for farmers with cows that had a lower fat content in their milk.

"My relatives were Holstein farmers so they got less money for their milk," Metzig says. "They were unhappy so they started their own co-op here. And they never did too well. They were always bugging the cheesemaker, so he would always quit. After five years, they sold it to my grandfather's brother. That was 1911, and then my grandfather's brother ran it as a private business. It was a pretty good sized factory in the '30s—there were three vats down there."

UNION STAR STRING CHEESE

In contrast to the stiff, dry, relatively flavorless experience of conventional string cheese, Union Star's product is moist and flavorful, like milk made solid and edible. Each fat, spaghetti-like cord is a tube of pure dairy essence, satisfyingly salty and tender.

A retail business and access to a prime country highway helped the plant thrive. "We were always retail oriented, which was unusual," Metzig says. "Most small cheese factories want to not have anything to do with people. Just somebody to back up a truck and load the cheese and take it away. And you don't have to put up with any of that complication. We were always retail oriented, and that is one of the reasons we survived."

In recent years, Metzig attributes the persistent success (or, in leaner years, survival) of his business at least in part to attitude. "What is the logic? I don't know if there is much," he says. "The basic skill in small business is to be really bull-headed. We are not brighter or harder working—we are mostly real persistent people. You just overcome hurdle after hurdle, and you have to be kind of mind-numbingly persistent."

Surviving in east central Wisconsin as a low-volume artisan cheesemaker, Metzig says, presents its own challenges. "The Fox Valley is kind of tough," Metzig says. "We don't have a single fresh produce store making it here, and there are four hundred thousand people, and we have a relatively good industrial base. The jobs are pretty good, but we are really kind of a tough German-type people. The supper clubs that make it are all-you-can-eat french fries and pitchers of beer—it's quite different than Minneapolis and Madison and Milwaukee. The upside," he adds, "is that they're very loyal through all the fads."

Distribution becomes a major challenge when working with a specialty product that needs to travel long distances. "You start running around twenty pounds of cheese at a time and the cost of distribution kills you," he says. "That is what you have to figure out, how to do that. And with enough oomph that it gets paid for in the system, it can be done."

David Metzig explains his plant's labor-intensive make procedure.

A skilled cheddar maker, Metzig has figured out how to make the most of any product he's not able to immediately distribute. "Aging is just something that happens to the stuff you don't sell," he says with a laugh. "Cheddar is a nice product where if you don't sell it as mild cheddar, you can raise the price and resell it as medium. If you don't sell it as medium, you raise the price and sell it as sharp. So you never panic. You get winters like this and you make cheddar."

Outside—for what seemed to be the hundredth day running—a light curtain of snow descended from billowing gray clouds.

The Masters

OF NORTHWESTERN WISCONSIN

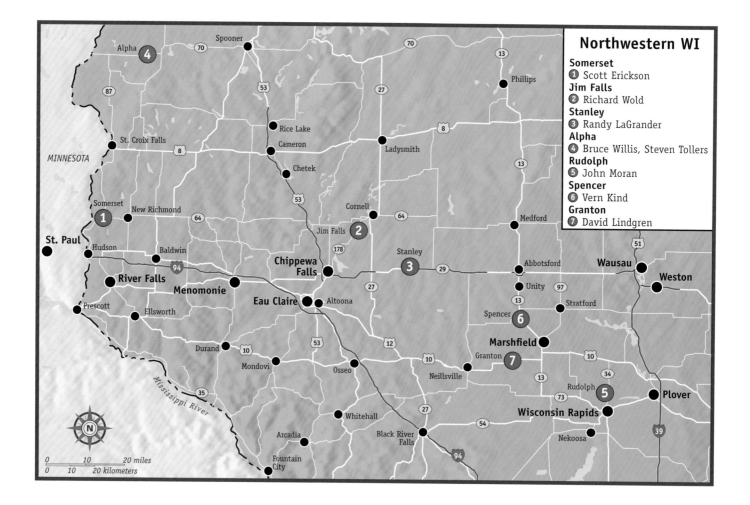

Northwestern WI

Somerset
1 Scott Erickson
Jim Falls
2 Richard Wold
Stanley
3 Randy LaGrander
Alpha
4 Bruce Willis, Steven Tollers
Rudolph
5 John Moran
Spencer
6 Vern Kind
Granton
7 David Lindgren

DISTANCES IN NORTHWESTERN WISCONSIN feel longer than in other parts of the state, the beginning of a process that meets its logical conclusion in the increasingly empty Plains and western states of North Dakota and Montana. The population starts to dwindle and spread out as you head north and west, moving toward the St. Croix and Mississippi rivers and away from the population centers of Milwaukee, Fox Valley, Madison, and Green Bay. It's not surprising, therefore, that northwestern Wisconsin has some cheese plants that are, in effect, community centers. The Burnett Dairy Cooperative in Alpha is halfway between Hudson and Superior, and it bustles with life and activity throughout the week. Bass Lake Cheese Factory (near Hudson) and the Wisconsin Dairy State Cheese Company (near Wausau) are also lively, with their sprawling shops that invite customers to stay awhile and browse, as is LaGrander's Hillside Dairy (near Chippewa Falls), with visitors as well as three generations of the LaGrander family working in the plant.

Some cheese giants do their work in this part of the state as well. Land O'Lakes (near Marshfield) and Associated Milk Producers, Inc. (near Chippewa Falls) deal with milk by the millions of pounds per day.

The northwestern part of the state is also the birthplace of colby, a venerable Wisconsin original cheese that was first created near the town of the same name. The cheese has its origins in the Steinwand Factory, opened in 1882, and although there is plenty of dispute as to the exact date and circumstances of its creation, the cheese—in its original form—was definitely a more moist and open-textured incarnation of cheddar. Real colby doesn't involve the labor-intensive cheddaring process that makes real cheddar such a bear to deal with, although it does involve an extra curd-washing step during the make. Four of the nine Wisconsin masters who claim colby among their areas of expertise live in the northwestern part of the state: John Moran, Bruce Willis, Randy LaGrander, and Scott Erickson.

Cinnamon-rubbed butter jack from Bass Lake Cheese Factory.

Scott Erickson

Bass Lake Cheese Factory, Somerset, Wisconsin
http://www.blcheese.com/

Master of cheddar, colby, monterey jack, muenster, and chèvre

*Knowing the different things you have to do to the milk, and that for every action there's a reaction,
and being able to manipulate those actions to produce different reactions is an art. It's not something you can
plug into a computer and plug into a piece of equipment.*

MASTER-LEVEL CHEESEMAKING HAPPENS ON MANY LEVELS. At one
extreme are the operations that process 2.5 million pounds of milk a day
and ship out cheese in fleets of tractor-trailers. At the other extreme is
the guy who carefully empties a nylon bag of delicate goat milk curd
into a stainless steel form. Scott Erickson of Bass Lake Cheese Factory is
the latter, a man of many hats who holds down the artisan end of the
master cheesemaker brotherhood.

Tattooed and slightly scruffy, wearing clothes more casual than the
starched, name-bedecked white uniform of a typical cheesemaker,
Erickson could easily be a sculptor or abstract painter. Fittingly, while
most master cheesemakers celebrate the artistic aspects of their work,
Erickson is almost consumed by them.

"I've always been really into art," he says. "That's one thing I
excelled in during my school years. Art's a way of expressing yourself,
and I feel pretty much the same thing about cheesemaking. One of

Scott Erickson of Bass Lake beats
partially made chèvre out of nylon bags to
prepare it for salting and aging.

Chèvre is left to dry for several days in nylon bags. Scott Erickson says the slow aging process gives his chèvre its smooth and mellow flavor.

the best compliments I ever got was from a professor at the University of Minnesota," Erickson says. "He was one of the main judges at the Minnesota State Fair. And when you sent your product in, they'd remove all the labels, and it would be comingled with hundreds of different cheeses. But he told me he could always identify which cheese came from here."

His plant at Bass Lake is small, but its retail operation—an increasingly large and critical part of the business strategy—sprawls over much of the building. It includes numerous coolers; an observation window overlooking the plant; walls of press clippings, medals, and prizes; and an extensive, informal cheesemaking museum.

The nod to cheese heritage is an interesting touch for Erickson, who is not a multigenerational maker. His beginnings are unique, at least among his fellow masters— he was hired by the Olsen Fish Company to make lutefisk, the gelatinous and pungent Norwegian holiday dish of lye-cured codfish. "In a sense it was still creating something in terms of using recipes that were old and handed down, and changing things a bit to make 'em your own," he says.

When the company bought the small Bass Lake plant near Somerset in the 1980s, the original plan was to compete with the big producers on their own turf: cheddar, colby, monterey jack. Erickson was brought in to help with the operation.

Economics soon dictated another strategy. In 1987 Erickson suggested a switch to goat cheese, an imported (typically French) luxury that was in scarce supply. "The hardest part was establishing a goat milk supply," Erickson says. "Most of [the farmers] were hobbyists. They really didn't understand the dairy industry or cleanliness, the sanitation aspects of it."

By working with patrons and state inspectors, Erickson was able to bring the quality of milk up to Wisconsin cheesemaking standards. After collaborating with the University of Minnesota on a chèvre recipe, Erickson soon attained success: "We got first place at the Minnesota State Fair with it, in 1989," he said. "That really broke through for us as far as the specialty cheese market." The breakthrough wasn't enough for his parent company, however, and soon afterward Erickson and his wife, Julie, wound up buying the plant, with the aid of a Small Business Administration loan.

After that, the floodgates opened. Chèvre was only the gateway cheese for Erickson, who is among the state's most creative specialty cheesemakers. He credits mentor Jim Path of the Center for Dairy Research with talking him into the master cheesemaker program, where his understanding of new cheeses blossomed. "He had the same kind of passion for new and unique European-style cheeses," Erickson says. "When you think about making cheese, it's basically taking a raw milk product and preserving it. And it's the physical things that you do, and the bacteria and cultures that you use, and the enzymes and different rennets that you use to create a preserved product that continues to age and get better. It's just short of a miracle," he adds. "It really excited me, and Jim Path had that same kind of passion that I had."

> **TASTING NOTES:**
> **BASS LAKE CHÈVRE**
>
> Chèvre is the product that really put Erickson and Bass Lake Cheese Factory on the map, and tasting it explains the appeal. It's a mild and delicate version, with a light (almost whipped) texture and clean, non-"goaty" finish spiked with a tangy stab of capronic acid.
>
> "It's always been a mainstay for us," says Erickson. "It's the one specialty cheese we've made that's successful and has always been successful, regardless of the economy."

A trip to Eastern Europe sponsored by the United States Agency for International Development also expanded Erickson's horizons. "Romania was the first country I got to go to," he says. "It was shortly after [Communist dictator Nicolae] Ceaușescu was overthrown [in 1989]. . . . They were trying to democratize the industry over there."

Erickson was tasked with teaching Romanians how to establish a privatized dairy industry. "One of the reasons I got picked is because we are such a small plant and we do everything by hand," he says. "You have to be innovative on what you use—they were very limited on equipment. I got to go over there and learn cheeses that had been made for thousands of years, and teach them what I knew, so they could produce product that was quality and safe to consume."

The trip was more grist for the mill, contributing to Bass Lake's current broad spread of specialty cheese. "All these things, up here [points to head] just kept feeding the fire in terms of making new cheeses," Erickson says. "We took old techniques, comingled them with new techniques, and just created new products."

Scott Erickson salts the chèvre before its final aging.

In addition to a number of different chèvre varieties (including one infused with truffles), the shop offers cheddars, cinnamon-rubbed butter jack, sheep mozzarella ("Ewezarella"), goat curds, and the Finnish specialty cheese juustoleipa.

Erickson is particularly proud of the last one, a fussy and unusual cheese little understood outside of the Finnish community. Bass Lake's juustoleipa passed a most unusual rite of passage.

"We went to FinnFest up in Hibbing, Minnesota," he says. "And if you don't know Finnish, you're kind of an outsider. And I don't know Finnish. Anyhow, we were sampling up there, among all these true Finnish people. And an elderly lady came up, and she was talking to—I assume it was her daughter—in Finnish, and her daughter translated that she wanted to try some juusto."

At this points, the stakes were raised.

"And then her daughter more or less scared me by saying, 'This better be good, because she makes it at home,'" he says. "So we had some warmed up, and she tries it, and turns around and walks off, and I thought, 'Oh, no.' And then she turns around and nods her head. It was the closest she'd come, from anything bought in the United States, to what it is in Finland."

Richard Wold

Associated Milk Producers, Inc. (AMPI), Jim Falls, Wisconsin

http://www.ampi.com/

Master of monterey jack and cheddar

We run 24/7 for 365 days out of the year.

"HOW'D I GET INTO CHEESEMAKING? I needed a job," quips Richard "Whitie" Wold, head of the cheese department at Associated Milk Producers, Inc.'s massive Jim Falls plant. His white hair at an early age inspired the nickname; it's emblazoned on his cheesemaker uniform.

"After high school, I went to trade school," he says. "I wasn't finding a job very easily. Some guys told me they were hiring in Jim Falls, so I drove up and put in an application. I drove home and then I got a call to come back for an interview. Basically they asked me if I wanted to work here, and I said sure. So they asked me if I could be in here at eleven o'clock that night. I was, and that's how it started."

Wold has worked every job in the cheese department at the Jim Falls plant, which is owned by a dairy co-op based in New Ulm, Minnesota, with more than four thousand midwestern farmers/owners. The plant goes through about 2.5 million pounds of milk a day, making it one of the biggest in the state.

Richard Wold stands in his two-level factory, where he developed his award-winning habañero jack cheese.

Unlike many of his master cheesemaker peers, Wold was originally a city boy. "I was born in Milwaukee, but both my parents were from around here," he says. "My dad was the head chef at the VA hospital in Milwaukee. But then my mother's uncle had a farm up here. I always liked coming up to visit, every summer ever since I was a little kid, as long as I can remember." There was always something to do on the farm, he recalled. "As I got older, my mom wouldn't let me move back. She said, 'You could be trouble.' She knew what she was talking about," he says.

Wold's habañero jack cheese recently won a second prize in its class at the 2008 World Championship Cheese Contest. Had it not been for his initiative, the plant's prize-winning variety would never have come into being.

"We were down at our Portage plant, looking at some other cheese," he says. "And I noticed he was buying pepper jack from a competitor. I came back and said, 'You know, guys, we can do that.' But the company would never give me the OK."

Wold got his green light to give it a try.

"So we made a vat, and they said it would be all right. We needed to improve on some things . . . so I talked to some other people about peppers, and it turned out the company we were buying peppers from was having problems because they were more stringy. We found nicer peppers, which we now buy by the truckloads in totes. We'll make three days of pepper jack in a week."

"Tote" is kind of a cute word to describe the massive, bulging containers of spicy vegetables that fill much of a large storage room in the plant. About 400 pounds of peppers—12 pails of jalapeños, or 11 of jalapeños and 1 of habañeros—go into each 5,200-pound table of spicy jalapeño or habañero jack cheese Wold makes. The habañero bags are smaller and more thickly packaged. Wold mentions that after handling habañeros, it's generally a good idea to wash up thoroughly before using the restroom.

"You learn that pretty quick," he adds with a laugh.

Despite decades of experience, Wold is modest about his career. When it's suggested that he knows a lot about cheese, he interjects immediately. "No, no, no, no . . . I'm still learning," he says. "Just from talking with [fellow masters], you learn. It was great to experience the camaraderie."

Wold expresses a bit of professional envy toward colleagues with the luxury to attend personally to each batch of cheese in process. At AMPI's scale, he says, production is relentless. "We make a vat of cheese every 22 minutes," he says. "We start pumping milk at 4:40 in the morning and get done pumping milk at 12:10 at

---

TASTING NOTES:
AMPI JALAPEÑO JACK

Unlike a number of jalapeño—and even habañero—jacks on the market, the AMPI version packs real heat. The flavor is well balanced, however, standing out from the mild, moist, creamy cheese without completely overwhelming it. Pleasant on its own, it's delicious on a cracker.

night. In that time, I'll push out something in the neighborhood of 260,000 pounds of cheese. And if something ain't quite working right, we gotta live with what's in that bucket. And then we've got to take care of it."

For all that pressure of production, Wold still finds time to play around with the product a bit. He has tried—and wishes he could regularly produce—a horseradish-infused variety of cheese. "I love to make it . . . but I can't clean the plant afterward," he says. Master cheesemaker Kerry Henning makes it, he adds. "He's small—he can do that kind of thing. He's got a picture on the wall, and there's three guys in gas masks. I said, 'Kerry, you're making horseradish.' He said, 'How do you know?' I said, 'It's right on the wall.' That's wicked stuff."

Jim Falls, Wisconsin.

Randy LaGrander

LaGrander's Hillside Dairy, Stanley, Wisconsin
http://www.lagranderscheese.com/

Master of colby, monterey jack, and cheddar

You cannot teach somebody to do it by a book. You need to have that hands-on experience.

Randy LaGrander shows off some of his plant's cheddar, matted midway through the cheddaring process.

IT'S PRETTY WELL UNDERSTOOD THAT CHEESEMAKING in Wisconsin is—or at least was—largely a family business. Fathers taught sons, referring back to what they'd learned from their own fathers and grandfathers. And while many Wisconsin plants have a generational story to them, few can—with a couple moments' notice and a bit of persuasive wrangling—assemble grandfather, father, and sons for a snapshot. This isn't just a portrait session; until interrupted, all the men were out on the floor, all dressed for work, all engaged in the art of making cheese.

"Both my parents were licensed cheesemakers," recalls Randy LaGrander, current plant chief of LaGrander's Hillside Dairy. "Years ago, in the 1950s, there were a lot of small farmer co-ops. And my parents used to run a lot of these co-ops for different people. Finally they decided: We're doing all this work, why don't we do it for ourselves? So they looked around central Wisconsin and finally settled on here. He bought this [plant] in 1960."

The plant that Dannie and Lorraine LaGrander built was also home until recently for the LaGrander family. Climb the stairs to the plant's upper level, and you discover a cheerful midwestern home disguised now as a conference room and a couple of offices.

"The convenience was nice," recalls LaGrander. "There was no travel. In the wintertime in a snowstorm you basically just walked down the steps."

The arrangement wasn't without its challenges, however.

"I remember growing up as a kid, and all the other kids were outdoors playing in the summertime and they had vacation, but you were always working," he says. "As a kid you think that's terrible. But it instills in you—all of our kids are very conscientious, and put everything into what they do."

LaGrander's wife, who still works in the plant on the business side of things, remembers the arrangement a little less nostalgically. Workers, she recalls, treated the house like an outbuilding, strolling up the stairs, storing milk in the fridge, and peering through the front door curtains to see who might be home.

Despite the pressures and occasional hassles of the cheese business, for LaGrander, there was never much question of choosing another line of work.

"I always enjoyed doing it," he says. "My personal thought was: Why do something else when you know you're going to come back here anyway? The younger you start the easier it is. My dad asked me if I wanted to get my license, and I was fifteen at the time. They had the [dairy] short course at Eau Claire, and he drove me back and forth to go to the classes and stuff, and I had my cheesemaking license before I had a driver's license."

When milk comes into LaGrander's plant, the liquid is efficiently harnessed at a level that would make an old corner plant owner's jaw drop. First, the milk is pasteurized and standardized for fat levels by adding nonfat milk solids. Standardized milk helps to produce consistent cheese.

"Then from the pasteurizer, the skim is added, and then it goes to the cheese vat and you add your ingredients," LaGrander says. "Then you add your rennet, set it up, and check your sets. . . . It's all cut, cooked, and it goes to the tables. . . . You remove half the whey from the vats so you don't have all that liquid."

The remainder of the whey is later pulled from the cheese-in-progress; it then goes to another storage tank, where butterfat is removed, and then onto another.

"Then we have to—to keep the quality of the whey—because you're full of enzymes—now you treat it just like milk," LaGrander says. "You repasteurize it to kill the cultures. Then it runs through the UF [ultra-filtration], which is a spiral membrane. Your protein molecules are larger than your other molecules, so that's how those get sifted out."

That protein then gets cooled and sold to another processor. Lactose (milk sugar) is taken out with a reverse osmosis system and, like the protein, sent to a dryer.

"Then the water gets sent to a water polisher to take off the organic materials, and then it goes to the polished tank which is better water than what you drink," he says. "Then we have two UV lights to kill any bacteria, then it goes to the storage tanks."

The 80- to 90-degree water is used to warm up the milk as it comes. The water, now cooled to about 50 degrees, is run back through the whey plate to cool the whey.

Three generations of LaGranders work at LaGrander's Hillside Dairy.
Center is Randy LaGrander, flanked by his sons, Joe and Ryan. Dannie stands behind him.

"We use all the water in one day—it gets used up in our wash-up systems," he says. LaGrander estimates that his system saves the plant about thirty thousand gallons in well water a day.

If the LaGrander plant's whey-handling system is firmly in the modern era, that's in keeping with Randy's tendency to keep an eye on the future of his business. That, in part, means getting his sons, Joe and Ryan, involved in the decision-making.

"I've got my way of doing things, but I try to be hands-off," he says. I'm really in the process of doing that now, trying to let them make some of their own decisions. They're going to make mistakes; you just try to limit them so they're not very costly," he says, laughing.

"All the kids are great kids. We haven't had any issues, knock on wood. I attribute that back to our lifestyle. Kids get into that urban mentality and they just get exposed to a lot of . . ." He pauses. "We're in the country, and it makes a world of difference."

LaGrander says that if you really want to see a country work ethic in action, the local Mennonite community is a good place to start.

"I went to haul a load of wastewater out to a farm, and there was a tractor in my way," he says. "I don't think the kid was much more than eight, ten years old. Black hat, pants, suspenders, a tool belt. . . . He jumps on his tractor, 100-horse tractor, starts it up running, and moves it out of the way for me. That's just how these kids grow up. By the time they're fifteen, sixteen years old, they're doing the majority of the work."

Bruce Willis and Steven Tollers

Burnett Dairy Cooperative, Alpha, Wisconsin
http://www.burnettdairy.com/

Masters of cheddar and colby (Willis), mozzarella and provolone (Tollers)

It all starts with the milk, farmers taking care of their cows. We've got the ultimate happy cows here.
—BRUCE WILLIS

Bruce Willis.

THOSE WHO WALK INTO THE Burnett Dairy Cooperative shop for the first time are likely to wonder what the special event is. Even on a weekday, the aisles are crowded; customers line up in front of the cheese coolers and mill around in front of the homespun-packaged muffin mixes and dehydrated soups that line the shelves.

"There was hardly anybody in there today," says Burnett cheesemaker Bruce Willis. "They'll get pretty packed in there, especially on the weekends. It's terrible," he deadpans.

The flip side of the community packing into the Highway 70 mainstay is that the factory's two master cheesemakers can get a sense of the buzz about their product. More likely than not, the buzz is good.

"You go up in the store, and you hear it a lot—someone will say, 'Where is this cheese? I got this cheese the other day, and this is the best cheese. I gotta have some of it,'" says Steven Tollers. "Just to see 'em, it's like being patted on the back."

Established as a creamery in 1896 and making cheese since 1966, Burnett has long concentrated on the Italian varieties that are its mainstay. In the 2008 World Championship Cheese Contest, the factory took home a best of class and second place for its aged provolone.

"Quantity, we don't care about that," says Tollers. "It's quality."

That quality is maintained even though the Burnett plant runs twenty-six million pounds of milk in a typical month, using a largely automated system.

Sometimes, says Willis, the ease of labor granted by that automated process presents its own challenges in terms of keeping the line running and churning out high-quality cheese. "You have to learn what to do if your automation breaks down," he says. "There's more to recover."

"Normally there's three vats in process at all times—one filling, one set, and one pumping over," says Tollers. "We had a little fun yesterday. We had a raccoon knock our power out, and *boom!* the whole plant was down."

"Then everybody scatters to reset everything," shares Willis.

"It was just a matter of minutes," says Tollers.

Willis, in a cool deadpan, adds, "We've had a few practice runs."

Willis has paved the way for the plant's new Wood River line of artisan cheeses, a name that hearkens back to half the plant's original identity; the Burnett Dairy Cooperative originated from a joining of the Branstad and Wood River creameries.

"We're not moving away from the Italian, we're just adding an artisan line," says Willis. "I got interested in it a few years ago. Taking those [master cheesemaker] classes down in Madison perked my interest in different things and blending cultures and enzymes, and kind of doing artistry with cheese science."

A Work Ethic on the Ropes

Talk to a cheesemaker today, and you're likely to hear common themes: the camaraderie of the profession, a need for quality over quantity, an interest in learning new things—and the fact that young people today don't know how to work. A retreat of rural values—and the relentless chores that used to be par for the course in Wisconsin's small towns and on its farms—is generally blamed.

"It's a shame. It's our generation that has taken that work ethic and given it to the TV," says Bruce Workman. "If you look at most of the kids, Mom and Dad spoon-feed them. That work ethic's not there. So it's gonna be tough to find somebody to replace us."

"The kids today don't have the work ethic that they had even twenty years ago," says David Lindgren. "A job is not high on the priority list. If they don't feel like getting up in the morning, that's my problem and it's not their problem, and it kind of sucks. They come in a couple hours late and they tell you you're lucky they're here."

"It's getting tough to find some young people to come in," says Steve Stettler. "They don't want the commitment. Friday night, they want to be gone."

Willis lights up when he describes some of the new cheeses rolling off the line. "There's a yogurt culture cheddar, and a blend called Alpha Morning Sun, which is kind of a cheddar/provolone/swiss-y blend. . . . It starts out a little sweet and nutty, but it's got a little Italian zing in it. We do different blends of things, just like when you're cooking. We've got a little experimental vat, so we can take a chance and take a risk. So far it's been turning out pretty good."

When asked about the co-op's booming business—it cleared more than $80 million in cheese sales in 2007, according to the *Inter-County Leader* of northwest Wisconsin—Willis credits the depth of experience possessed by the plant's team of cheesemakers. "We probably have six cheesemakers here with thirty years of experience each. There isn't much we don't know. And we have some with twenty years, and another bunch now who just started."

As for the work ethic among the younger people, Willis isn't as pessimistic as some of his colleagues at other plants. "It varies," he says. "It depends on where they come from. You see a lot of variation. Before, everyone came from a farm or worked on a farm. But now, you might've come from helping around a neighborhood farm, or odd jobs, or you might've come from behind a video game machine."

Steve Tollers.

Computer skills are, of course, relevant at a plant like Burnett, which relies on a good deal of automated equipment to make the cheese. At the same time, the plant's reliance on old-fashioned, labor-intensive cheddaring helps get the new workers acculturated to the industry's standard of hard work.

"It kind of opens the younger guys' eyes when you tell 'em this is how we did it all day long," Willis says. "They go: 'Noooo . . .'"

Tollers lights up at the mention of cheddaring, flashing back to his early days in the business. "We raced each other all day," he says. "It was kind of a competition—the guy across the table would start cheddaring, and you'd think, 'Let's see who's got the most steam.'"

Tollers got into cheesemaking after a four-year stint in the Marine Corps, so his gung-ho attitude makes a certain amount of sense. But it wasn't a fondness for back-breaking labor that kept him in the cheese business for more than three decades. "It was fun doing it," he says. "I got to see the cause and effect—you take milk and add a culture to it and coagulant and you get something like pudding that you turn into cheese. Quite interesting."

Tollers credits the challenge of learning more about cheesemaking with getting him into the master cheesemaker program. "I guess I like a challenge," he says. "You got people out there saying, 'You can't do this, you can't do that.' Well, I can do it. And that's the type of challenge I wanted to get into, and I took the challenge, and I'm glad I did. It's a title, too," he adds. "There's a lot of people out there who look up to it. You say 'master cheesemaker,' and you wouldn't believe how many people comment on that."

Given a little time to consider further, Tollers mentions another key to the appeal of the master program: "The camaraderie, like at the World Cheese Show we were just at," he says. "I was sitting down for lunch the first day, and Bruce Workman sits down. . . . All the master cheesemakers have the thing where if you're wearing your ring, you go and click rings. It's kind of like your own little group of guys there."

Steve Tollers and Bruce Willis stand in the Burnett Dairy Cooperative cheese plant.

Cows near Stanley, Wisconsin.

John Moran

Wisconsin Dairy State Cheese Company, Rudolph, Wisconsin
phone (715) 435-3144

Master of cheddar and colby

When there's a family function, two can go, and one has to stay here. That is part of the family business.
One of us has to stay back just in case something happens.

SOME WISCONSIN CHEESE PLANTS don't deal with retail operations. Customers can be a hassle—they introduce a whole new layer of work to the business. Other plants have retail stores, but they're deliberately small, just a counter and a list of prices.

Then there are stores—fewer than you might hope—that throw their doors open to the community. Stop by the Wisconsin Dairy State Cheese Company in Rudolph, and you can buy one of dozens—perhaps hundreds—of cheeses for sale. You can hang out at one of the comfortable tables and watch cheese being made through the massive picture window that dominates the room. And you can munch on an ice-cream cone made with Chocolate Shoppe Ice Cream, one of Madison's finest premium dairy exports.

"The cash sales here was dad's gift back to the dairy industry," master cheesemaker John Moran says. "He always liked talking to people and seeing people and having people coming in—it's basically advertising. You give a good product for a reasonable price, and it keeps people coming back."

CHEESE CURDS

The squeaky, salty, milky, sometimes deep-fried treats known as cheese curds are not typical of most of the curd used in the pressing and making of cheese. They're typically the result of the old-fashioned cheddaring process, which uses the stacking, cutting, and milling of melted curd to produce drier, more substantial curds that make for good aged cheddar or straight-up snacking.

Curds go downhill in quality fairly quickly, losing their putty-like texture, moisture, and natural squeak. Many cheese plants rush a batch out the door fairly early in the morning, such that the stores and gas stations they supply have curds on hand that are typically no more than a day or two old.

Community and family come up time and time again when Moran talks about his work. "We still have a core group of friends here for Easter, Thanksgiving, and Christmas," Moran says. "They still come back home, and it's nothing for anywhere from five to ten couples to go out. We keep in touch."

The cheese plant and its friendly, open retail space help keep people connected. "Friends from the grade ahead of me and friends from the grade behind me come to the cheese factory," Moran says. "If they want to get in touch with somebody and they're not sure how to do it, they'll ask, because maybe I can give them a lead."

The setup helps the plant keep in touch with its dairy patrons, as well. "With our cash sales, a lot of our farmers are our friends," he adds. "We have one of the most beautiful cash sales you'll ever see, run by Jill, my sister, and father, Mike. With the nice observation windows, when they come in, they'll wave or we'll wave, or we'll go out and we'll talk. Sometimes we'll talk about farming, sometimes we'll talk about deer hunting or

John Moran.

fishing, or sometimes we'll talk about the crops or the weather, you know. . . . It's just nice to see 'em."

The plant's community roots run deep. Moran's grandfather worked at the factory back in the '40s, and bought it when it was little bigger than a ranch house. "It was basically a make room, a boiler, and that kind of stuff—it was very small," Moran says. "He had some sons and daughters and, well, that was back in the late 1940s, early '50s. He started Wisconsin Dairy State Cheese Company. Then in the 1960s, his two sons—Mike, who's my father, and Dave—became part of the ownership."

As Mike and Dave got older and more experienced, the plant grew with them. "We started adding on, and adding on, and in the late 1970s we actually built a brand new cheese factory," Moran says. "Then when we built a new cheese factory, we went from the old make method of the open vats to the Double O's and finishing tables and that kind of stuff—we went with the modern technology. Before that, we were one of the first plants in the U.S. to ever R.O. and U.F. whey."

Reverse osmosis and ultrafiltration of whey are seen by many cheesemakers as a critical commercial edge—for some, it's the difference between prospering and failure. Demand for whey-derived proteins, like many other commodities in an increasingly overheated market, has soared in recent years.

Family input is critical to keeping the plant running, says Moran. "It's nice working with my dad, working with my uncle, working with my cousin, working with my sister—you know," Moran says. Then he pauses. "One thing with Dad is—it's like he has eyes behind his head," he says with a laugh. "He's very fussy. That's a good thing. There's only one way to do it, and that's the right way. The thing is, he's not afraid to get on his hands and knees and make sure things are being cleaned. That's one unique thing about our plant: our jobs all overlap. Nothing ever gets out of hand. If something's going to happen, we catch it right away. That's unique." The result is Wisconsin cheese made with a Wisconsin family work ethic.

"We specialize in cheddar and colby and monterey jack," Moran says. "Those are the most popular ones. And everything we make we sell to one large company with the exception of what we sell here at our cash sales. I think some of the more rewarding things are . . . well, the good people we work with—but when you start making a piece of cheese from when it's just milk, into the vat, and then onto the finishing table—being able to see it from start to finish and then being able to cut it. That's, you know, a good piece of cheese. That's very rewarding."

John Moran demonstrates his factory's controls.

Vern Kind

LAND O'LAKES, Spencer, Wisconsin
http://www.landolakes.com/

Master of cheddar

My favorite part of the job is working with plant people, working on projects,
and if the project is successful—you hit a home run, so to speak—that's rewarding.

WHEN THE AVERAGE PERSON HEARS THE TERM "master cheesemaker," a common first inclination is to imagine a guy leaning over a stainless steel or copper vat making a hand-crafted batch of cheese. In one sense, that might describe Land O'Lakes senior scientist Vern Kind to a T. He's got a small test operation set up in one of the firm's Arden Hills office complexes, and has the opportunity to play with cheese on a small scale whenever it's necessary.

But for Kind, actual cheesemaking is only one component of his daily duties, which can broadly be defined as "serving as a general purpose cheesemaker ninja troubleshooter who parachutes in wherever there's trouble."

"Part of my job is that I get around to look at lots of different cheese plants across the country, and I really enjoy that," he says. "Not only do I work with our Land O'Lakes plants, but people who copack and make cheese for us. So I get to see lot of different operations and meet a lot of people. The most rewarding part of the job right now is getting to meet other people in the industry and getting to know them better. Before you'd meet them at a cheesemaker's convention and not really get to know them. Now I get out to some of the plants and actually work with people, and that's been great."

Vern Kind and a display of products made by Land O'Lakes.

In contrast to the farmstead cheesemaker who literally works from home, Kind is a road warrior. "A typical week in the Midwest, I might spend a couple days in the Spencer plant, and then spend a couple days up here [in Arden Hills]," he says. "Then we've got two plants in Denmark and Kiel, Wisconsin. We've got plants in Minnesota and I regularly go up there. We've got a couple cheese plants out in California. Usually I go out there and spend a week at a time.

"Every plant is different," he adds. "That's a challenging thing, and not everybody understands that. They think: You should plop in a recipe, and if it works in one plant, it should work everywhere. But every plant has unique equipment, layout . . . they're all different. And there are a lot of live organisms involved."

Kind's work never ends, as Land O'Lakes, a massive agricultural cooperative with billions of dollars in annual sales, makes a lot of cheese. "It's in the hundreds of millions of pounds of cheese a year," he says. "It's a lot of cheese."

Kind got his start at a small plant called Greenwood Milk Products in Greenwood, Wisconsin, running a couple hundred thousand pounds of milk a day. Over the years, says Kind, cheese production has shifted from small plants (many of which have shuttered their doors) to larger, more consolidated operations.

"Certainly the operations have gotten much larger," he says. "And that's certainly true with

Vern Kind stands in a Land O'Lakes test factory.

the farmers. They've gotten larger and there's fewer of them. There are fewer plants. Used to be in Wisconsin there was cheese plants every few miles, because there just wasn't the means to ship milk very far."

Better transportation and information infrastructure have meant that competition has developed a longer reach, an evolution that has changed the way cheesemakers view their business world. "The dairy industry has gotten more global—there's competition even within the United States," he says. "You see a lot more competition with cheeses from California and Idaho and even New Mexico, so that's been a big change for the dairy industry, too."

Kind still sees an edge for Wisconsin cheese, however—years of experience and a state history enmeshed with dairy production. Generational knowledge, he says, makes for a special kind of craftsperson. "They're more the elite and the artisan cheesemakers because they have the experience," he says. "You get out to the West Coast and they're more the commodity, high volume type plants. The specialty plants you generally see in Wisconsin. Out West, the emphasis tends to be on high volume and 'get it out the door.'"

With Kind's schedule, you'd think he might stick close to home for recreation. But when we caught up with him in early 2008, he was just about ready to leave for Alaska.

"Going fishing?" we asked.

"I'm actually going bear hunting," he said.

"What do you do with the bear?" we asked.

"Hopefully you shoot him before he gets you," he responded, more calmly than you might expect.

A sign near Granton advertising the joys of dairy products.

David Lindgren

LYNN DAIRY, Granton, Wisconsin
http://www.lynndairy.com/

Master of mozzarella, provolone, cheddar, and monterey jack

I knew that I wanted to get into the management level. I wasn't going to be happy just as a floor cheesemaker.

DRIVE DEEP ENOUGH INTO AMISH COUNTRY near Granton and Neillsville, on Highway 10, and you'll stumble across Lynn Dairy. Or, more accurately, you'll first stumble across a depot where men are lugging heavy metal cans of milk out of trucks and then pulling them back out again through a side entrance high enough to make truck loading a little easier.

Lynn Dairy is one of the few dairies in the state that deals with Amish milk.

"We're bringing in over sixty thousand pounds of Amish milk a day," says plant manager and master cheesemaker David Lindgren. "Loyal, Granton, and Greenwood are huge Amish communities, so that's where we do most of our volume. You gotta be careful early in the morning and in the evening, because there are a lot of horses and buggies on the road."

Moving and cooling canned milk present unique challenges. "We bring the cans in, it's immediately dumped into a hanging stainless steel scale and dumped onto a cooling plate and storage tank and taken here," Lindgren says. "The Amish, of course, can only cool it to well-water temperature. If you get fifty-degree milk, you're doing pretty well. A lot of times it's sixty degrees or over, so you've got to get it in and get it cooled right away."

Although the milk requires extra care, it's of exceptional quality. "It's actually a hand-milked cow, which doesn't go through as much stress as an automated system where they're wheelin' 'em into a parlor, throwin' 'em on and takin' 'em off," says Lindgren. "There's a little more tender loving care."

Lindgren says the butterfat and protein levels—two of the key components to determining the usefulness of milk—are particularly high in Amish milk. "The only time you have a hard time is July and August when it's eighty and you have a hard time cooling it," he says. "We end up dumping a lot because we have quality systems up there, too. And then you have to go through the whole thing of picking it up. It gets dumped and they don't get paid for it."

Lindgren turns the Amish (and conventional) milk into a variety of cheeses, mostly American in style. But he's an experienced Italian cheesemaker, as well. "I am a master cheesemaker in Italian cheeses—which I did, through Arpin Dairy—then I got here and went back into American cheeses. So I've got the [master's certifications in] cheddar, monterey jack, the provolone, and the mozz. Most of my awards have been through the provolone and mozzarella string cheese through Arpin. Obviously I've only been here for five years, so I don't have that many awards racked up. Not yet."

David Lindgren.

His biggest award and proudest moment was winning a best in class for his provolone cheese at the United States Championship Cheese Contest in 1997. "I know the year because it was the year the Packers won the Super Bowl," he says. "So my cheese was actually displayed with Brett Favre on that poster." The poster he mentions is one that you'll see in a lot of offices and break rooms in Wisconsin cheese plants. It features the Green Bay quarterback standing amid a sea of cheese. The text reads: "Champions: Green Bay Packers and Wisconsin Cheese, 1997 United States Champion Cheeses from Wisconsin."

Despite the dairy's tight connection with small farmers, it's grown massively since Lindgren's arrival. When Lindgren arrived in 2003, the plant was running five hundred thousand pounds of milk a day, for four days a week. "Now we're running a million two a day, six days a week," he says. "It's grown a lot just in the last four and a half years."

Business is too good, to the point of being a little wild. "If anything, I've got an issue with shipping cheese out too fresh," he says. "Which is a good problem. You always want to wait until you've got your lab analyticals before you ship it out the door, so sometimes you have to say, 'No, that can't go out Monday, it's got to be Tuesday.'"

It's all part of the plant's aggressive approach to quality control. "I guess the most rewarding thing for me is seeing that truck being loaded with good quality cheese," he says. "That and knowing that it has a label on it that reads 'Lynn Dairy' and that I can be proud of it."

A horse enjoys the arrival of spring outside of Jim Falls.

Other Masters

THE AUTHORS WERE ABLE TO INTERVIEW and photograph forty-three of the forty-four master cheesemakers active as of winter 2007–8. That leaves one active master and six other program graduates who deserve recognition.

ALLAN SCOTT (Saputo Cheese USA) is certified in low-moisture/part-skim mozzarella and provolone cheeses, and works in Saputo's tech service group in Lena, Wisconsin. Scott originally worked at a cheese plant in Kent, Illinois, but the master cheesemaker program influenced his decision to move up to Wisconsin to pursue his certification. Scott hopes to fully explore the possibilities of mozzarella by earning future certifications in whole-milk and reduced-fat mozzarella.

WALT BRANDLI (Babcock Hall Dairy Plant, retired) made cheese at the university's Babcock dairy plant from 1992 until 2004, obtaining master certifications in brick, cheddar, baby swiss, and gouda. Before going to Babcock, he operated his own cheese factory in Mauston, Wisconsin, for more than thirty years. He passed away at his home in Madison on June 29, 2007, at age seventy-four.

JEROME ZIBROWSKI (Mindoro Co-op Creamery, retired) mastered in the blue and gorgonzola cheeses that Mindoro became nationally famous for in the late '90s. He graduated from high school in 1984 on a Friday and was working full time at the Mindoro Co-op Creamery the following Monday, influenced in part by his father, who was the plant's manager. He found the transition to blue-veined cheeses initially difficult, but he eventually mastered them with award-winning results.

RANDY KRAHENBUHL (Fair Oaks Farms of Indiana) produced an aged gouda that was selected as the Cheese and Butter Grand Champion of the 2007 World Dairy Expo. A Wisconsin native, he owned and operated Monticello's Prima Käse Cheese before moving to Indiana in 2001. Krahenbuhl was encouraged in his career by Green County cheesemaking legend Albert Deppeler, and at one time he was the only cheesemaker in the United States making traditional 180-pound wheel swiss in copper kettles. He obtained master certifications in swiss and gouda, and he is credited with creating Sweet Swiss cheese, a sweeter, creamier variation of traditional swiss.

BOB BIDDLE (Swiss Valley Farms, retired) mastered in swiss and, in a CDR *Dairy Pipeline* article, cited his dad as a guiding influence. "I think he forgot more about making cheese than I know," he told the *Pipeline*. Cheesemaking was part of Biddle's life from an early age—he recalls watching his father make cheese from the vantage point of an unused ten-thousand-pound open vat that served as his playpen. About the craft of making swiss cheese, Biddle told the Wisconsin Milk Marketing Board that "striving for good eye formation, body, and flavor can be a nerve-racking but fulfilling process."

DAN MEISTER (Meister Cheese Company, retired) obtained his master certifications for monterey jack and cheddar in 1999, having spent decades working at his family's plant in Muscoda, Wisconsin, now on its third generation of owner-operators. His family's roots in the business date back to Grandpa Joe Meister, who started the cheesemaking dynasty in Plain, Wisconsin, in 1923. A world traveler, Meister journeyed to Europe to demonstrate cheesemaking, and, in 1997 and 1998, he accompanied his mother to Bosnia, where she regularly traveled to deliver medical supplies to refugee camps. A pioneer in the repurposing of whey, Meister also founded Muscoda Protein Products.

RON SULLIVAN (Swiss Valley Farms, retired) has a certification in swiss cheese, but he no longer makes cow's milk cheeses. Sullivan had a long career at Swiss Valley Farms/Old Wisconsin Cheese, getting his start in 1981. He is one of many Wisconsin cheesemakers with ties to the Jenny family of Platteville, Wisconsin—fifty-two-year cheesemaking veteran Clarence Jenny of the former Platteville Dairy encouraged Sullivan to get his license.

GLOSSARY OF CHEESEMAKING TERMS

affinage: Simply put, the aging or finishing of a cheese after it has been made and pressed into shape. Affinage can require a number of steps intended to precisely manipulate temperature and humidity and the application of flavoring, such as olive oil, wine, or cocoa powder. Made and stored properly, some varieties of cheese can comfortably age for years, acquiring sharper and more complicated flavors as time goes by.

annatto: A dye derived from achiote trees (from tropical regions of the Americas), used to give Wisconsin cheeses such as cheddar and colby their distinctive yellow color.

bloomy rind: A surface mold common to many softer cheeses, such as brie, camembert, and brillat-savarin. Sometimes called blooming rind.

brining: The soaking of cheese in salt-saturated water, which adds flavor, affects rind texture, and acts as a drying agent.

CDR: The Wisconsin Center for Dairy Research, a joint initiative of the University of Wisconsin and the Wisconsin Milk Marketing Board. CDR acts as a conduit for transmitting information between working dairymen and cheesemakers in the field and experts in the scientific world.

cheddaring: A labor-intensive process used to drive moisture out of cheddar curd. It can be used to create either ready-to-eat cheese curds or quality aged cheddar. By heating, stacking, cutting, restacking, recutting, and finally milling the initial cheddar curd, much of the whey is removed from the finished cheese.

co-op: Typically a joint operating agreement between a group of dairy farmers and a cheesemaker. For example, the cheesemaker might make the cheese and own the equipment, while the dairy farmers own the cheese plant and supply the milk, sharing the profits and risk according to a predetermined formula.

curd: The bulk of the proteins and fat found in milk, coagulated into a semisolid mass that is the basis for most kinds of cheese. Further along in the process, if the cheesemaker chooses to cheddar, mill, and salt the curd, it becomes cheese curds, which are sold as a snack food.

make: Short for "make procedure," the overall method used for making a given cheese.

microfauna: A generic term for the various bacteria, molds, and viruses that can either hinder or assist the cheesemaking process.

mixed milk: A cheese made with more than one sort of animal milk, such as cow's milk mixed with sheep's milk.

organic milk: Milk labeled "USDA Organic" from cows that have not been treated with bovine growth hormone (BGH), which boosts production. In addition, according to vague federal guidelines, the cows should have "access to pasture" and eat pesticide-free feed.

pasta filata: Italian term (literally "spun paste") referring to a specific step in the manufacture of such Italian cheeses as mozzarella and provolone. Heating, kneading, and stretching give the cheese its distinctive elastic and soft texture.

pasteurized: Milk that has been brought up to a temperature (typically 161°F) for fifteen seconds, high enough and long enough to kill the existing bacteria.

pH: The measure of the acidity or alkalinity of a solution. Because acidity can have a crucial impact on the quality of the final product, makers carefully monitor and control the pH of their cheese as it's made.

phage: Short for "bacteriophage," a kind of virus that infects bacteria. Phage can neutralize a starter culture and shut down the making of a vat of cheese.

rBGH: Synthetically produced bovine growth hormone used to boost milk production in cows. rBGH is controversial for health risks it presents to animals as well as potential health risks to milk consumers.

rennet: An enzyme, typically derived from a calf stomach or a plant such as thistle, that causes milk to separate into curds and whey.

rind: The exterior of a cheese. Rinds are often edible, particularly in softer cheeses.

smear: A bacterial broth used to ripen cheese during the aging process.

starter culture: Bacteria cultivated to consume and transform various components (such as sugars and proteins) of the milk (and cheese) during the cheesemaking process, thereby giving cheeses their distinctive flavor and texture.

stirred curd: A cheesemaking method that typically uses an automated metal stirring device to agitate the curd. It's one of the essential processes for making many kinds of cheese, and in cheddar specifically it can be used as a stand-in for traditional cheddaring.

trier: A T-shaped stainless steel tool used to take long sample plugs out of wheels or blocks of cheese.

washed rind: A type of cheese that is, during the aging process, washed with a solution of water and bacteria to promote ripening and flavor development.

whey: The watery, still-protein-rich element of milk cast off after the curd is coagulated. Whey has many uses, such as protein supplements or pet food additives.

WISCONSIN CHEESE ON THE WEB

Center for Dairy Research: http://www.cdr.wisc.edu/
   Information on dairy courses, a newsletter (*Dairy Pipeline*), and brief bios of the CDR's talented staff.

Cheese Underground: http://www.cheeseunderground.blogspot.com/
   Frequently updated posts featuring special events and classes, detailing plant openings, profiling noteworthy new cheeses, and generally exploring the progress of the Wisconsin dairy industry.

Dairy Business Innovation Center: http://www.dbicusa.org/
   A deep resource for specialty and artisan dairy entrepreneurs.

Master Cheesemaker Book Blog: http://mastercheesemakerbook.wordpress.com/
   Expanded material uncovered during the researching of this book, including photos, sound clips, news reports, cheese-tasting notes, and more.

Wisconsin Cheesemakers Association: http://www.wischeesemakersassn.org/
   A good place to visit for cheese contest results and scheduling information.

Wisconsin Dairy Artisan Network: http://www.wisconsindairyartisan.org/
   A place for current and future dairy artisans to obtain help with craft, business, and regulatory questions.

Wisconsin Master Cheesemaker Directory: http://www.eatwisconsincheese.com/wisconsin/masters/default.aspx
   Searchable directory with current capsule biographies and photos of Wisconsin's master cheesemakers, plus background on the program itself.

Wisconsin Milk Marketing Board: http://www.eatwisconsincheese.com/
   A veritable treasure trove of cheese information, including tour guides, cheese pairings, a cheese of the week, cheese videos, and more.

SOURCES

In addition to conducting the more than fifty interviews on which this book is primarily based, the authors consulted numerous periodicals and the following publications:

Apps, Jerry. *Cheese: The Making of a Wisconsin Tradition*. Amherst, WI: Amherst Press, 1998.

Federal Writers' Project. *The WPA Guide to Wisconsin*. New York: Duell, Sloane, and Pearce, 1941.

Freeman, Sarah. *The Real Cheese Companion*. London: Time Warner, 1998.

Hintz, Martin, and Pam Percy. *Wisconsin Cheese: A Cookbook and Guide to the Cheeses of Wisconsin*. Guilford, CT: ThreeForks, 2008.

Hoard's Dairyman: The National Dairy Farm Magazine. Online at http://hoards.com/history/chronology.html.

Jenkins, Steven. *Cheese Primer*. New York: Workman Publishing, 1996.

Lampard, Eric E. *The Rise of the Dairy Industry in Wisconsin: A Study in Agricultural Change, 1820–1920*. Madison: State Historical Society of Wisconsin, 1963.

Marquis, Vivienne, and Patricia Haskell. *The Cheese Book*. New York: Simon & Schuster, 1965.

McCalman, Max, and David Gibbons. *Cheese: A Connoisseur's Guide to the World's Best*. New York: Clarkson Potter, 2005.

McGee, Harold. *On Food and Cooking: The Science and Lore of the Kitchen*. New York: Scribner, 2004.

Selitzer, Ralph. *The Dairy Industry in America*. New York: Magazines for Industry, 1976.

Wisconsin Cartographers' Guild. *Wisconsin's Past and Present: A Historical Atlas*. Madison: University of Wisconsin Press, 1998.

INDEX